M.

For Kel —
May you enjoy
these gathered words.
Merry Christmas 2022,
ILY!
Me ♥

vol. 3

THE MOLEHILL: VOLUME THREE
© 2014 Rabbit Room Press

Published with care and diligence by:
RABBIT ROOM PRESS
3321 Stephens Hill Lane
Nashville, Tennessee 37013
info@rabbitroom.com

Edited by A. S. Peterson
Cover concept & design by Jason McFarland

Warning: The diligent reading of this book has been known to cause blindness in parakeets.

ISBN 978-0-9889632-9-0
FIRST EDITION
Printed in the United States of America
14 15 16 17 18 19— 6 5 4 3 2 1

RABBIT ROOM
— PRESS —

the MOLEHILL

volume 3

e collibus montes

Contents

PLAYING AS A TEAM
by A. S. Peterson, Editor

This book, like those before it, has been a lot of work, and, more importantly, a lot of fun. The work comes with the territory. No surprise there. But the fun? The fun is in working with so many people I love and watching them stretch themselves in new and exciting ways. The fun is in watching them play and create and grow together. I can think of no work more enjoyable than that of creating in the company of good friends.

A journal like this is a group effort, and not only because the contributor list is robust, but because it's created not merely by me or by Rabbit Room Press, but by *us*—the writers. I see or speak with most of the included writers on a regular basis, and not usually for work. Often it's just for waffles. We discuss what we're writing, we bounce ideas around, we laugh, we play, we go home and write. This book is a community in print that represents a community in flesh and blood.

With this third volume in particular, I'm delighted to see so much collaboration evident right here in these pages. Contributions like those of Jen Rose Yokel and Jonny Jimison, who have collaborated on an original piece of cartoon poetry, might not have happened outside of the communal round-table of the Rabbit Room. Lewis Graham has been a guest in our home and an integral part of our lives for the past few years, and now his recipes are wonderfully illuminated by my wife's illustrations. Jonny Jimison also provides the illustration for my own included short story. And the poetry of Chris and Jen Yokel seems something of a meta-collaboration as the poems themselves are individual creations written by two parts of a collaborative life: a husband and wife.

And of course the editorial process itself is a team effort. We push and pull and wrestle with one another's words, hoping to pin the best of them down for you to read. It's hard work, but it's good work. All this is a joy to me as a writer, because writing is so often a solitary sport. *The Molehill* gathers us into a team, and it really does feel like playing. It's that much fun. And isn't that how it should be? I see no reason why not.

A. S. Peterson
Editor, *The Molehill*

vol. 3

THE BLACK HORIZON (PART I)
Story and Illustrations by Jamin Still

THE HOURGLASS

Jacob's father craned his neck as he looked up at the tower. The light from the rising sun was just touching the top of the spire. "What an adventure, eh? Maybe even a Great Adventure." He reached down and patted Jacob's shoulder then read from the scrap of paper in his hand. "*Up and down again before the sun sets, and whatever you desire shall be yours.* Not everyone gets one of these, you know," he said, holding up the paper. "We need this, son. And you can do it, with time to spare. I would do it myself, but . . ." He looked down at his twisted leg and tapped it with his cane and sighed. "Go on, now. I'll wait here."

The boy shook a little, his feet rooted to the ground. He *could* do it, he supposed. But of course it wasn't as simple as going up and coming down, not if half the stories about The Hourglass were true. And if they *were* true and he *was* delayed, and the sun slipped beneath the horizon before he emerged—Jacob didn't like to think what that would mean. He eyed the yellowed parchment in his father's hand and wished again it had not come to them.

But if he *did* do this thing, if he embarked on this Great Adventure and succeeded . . . He imagined his father's face—the absence of disappointment—and this made him shake a little less. *What I desire* will *be mine*, he thought.

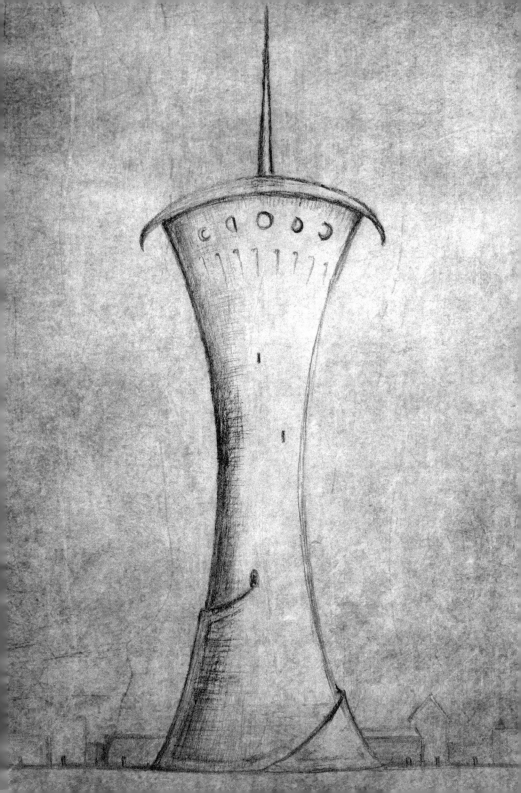

"All right," said Jacob. He took the paper from his father and without looking back he walked across the square, up the spiraling stair, and entered The Hourglass.

When he emerged from the tower nine hours later, the sun was just above the western horizon. Jacob was battered and bleeding, and he shook, but this time with excitement. He shaded his eyes and looked eagerly out across the square. But of his father there was no sign.

When he arrived home, the house was dark and his father's bag was gone.

REMBRANDT IS IN THE WIND
by Russ Ramsey

Think of how bored they get, stacked
in the warehouse somewhere, say in Mattapan,
gazing at the back of the butcher paper
they are wrapped in, instead of at
the rapt glad faces of those who love art.
Only criminals know where they are.
The gloom of criminality enshrouds them.[1]

—John Updike

THE HEIST

The security guard sitting behind the main desk of the Isabella Stewart Gardner Museum looked up from his homework when he heard the buzzer for the Palace Road entrance. On the monitor he saw two uniformed police officers standing outside. Through the intercom, the officers told him they had received a report of a disturbance in the museum's courtyard and needed to check it out.

---

[1] From John Updike's poem, *Stolen*, 2000

It was 1:24am on March 19, 1990. Though midnight officially marked the end of St. Patrick's Day, the pubs in Boston's Fenway neighborhood were still pouring pints and spilling their staggering celebrants into the streets when, against protocol, the guard buzzed the officers in.

Once inside, the officer in charge asked the guard if he had noticed anything unusual and if there was anyone else on duty that night.

The guard told them yes, he had a partner upstairs and no, they had not seen anything out of the ordinary.

The lead officer said, "Go ahead and call your partner down here."

The second officer studied the guard's face as he made the call.

"You look familiar," the second officer said to the guard. "Is there a warrant out for your arrest?"

The security guard looked surprised and insisted there wasn't, but the question itself set him on edge and his denial seemed only to deepen the officer's suspicion.

"Please come over here and show me your ID," the lead officer ordered.

The security guard stepped out from behind the desk and away from the only silent alarm button in the museum. He handed his driver's license and Berklee College of Music ID to the officer. After studying the license for a second the officer cuffed the guard and said, "You are under arrest. We need to take you in."

Just then the second watchman on duty that night, an aspiring musician, came around the corner and the officers immediately put him in handcuffs too.

Surprised, the second guard asked, "Why are you arresting me?"

The officers said, "You are not being arrested. You are being robbed. Don't give us any problems and you won't get hurt."

The thieves then bound the guards, covered their eyes and mouths with tape, and chained them to pipes on opposite ends of the basement. After this, the thieves spent the next eighty-one minutes selecting and loading thirteen irreplaceable pieces of art into a vehicle waiting outside.

Then they drove off quietly past the homes and businesses of Fenway, never to be heard from again.

THE STORM

The sea surges and swells. The little fishing boat has no hope of holding on to the churnching foam below. The bow rides up the back of one white breaker while the stern dips into the valley beneath it. Waves break over the sides. The half dozen men to Rembrandt's right shout and strain at the sails, struggling to keep the ship from capsizing. The five men to his left plead with Jesus of Nazareth to save them. Rembrandt stands in the middle of the boat, his right hand tightly clutching a rope and his left pinning his hat to his head. His name is scrawled across the useless rudder, as though this is his boat on his sea and they are all caught in his storm. He and everyone else in the ship are soon to be lost unless their leader intervenes.

We don't think much about our mortality, but the question is never far away. It comes in an instant and often brings with it an inherent sense of reverence. Life is a fragile, sacred thing. This sacred fragility has played a central role the creation of much of the world's great art. We marvel at the lithe physical perfection of youth in Michelangelo's *David*.[2] We wonder what sort of burden has Rodin's *Thinker*[3] so bent over.[4] We avert our eyes from death in Reuben's *The Lamentation Over the Dead Christ*,[5] as Joseph of Arimathea and Nicodemus lay Jesus's lifeless body on a stone slab.

When our seas are calm, we regard them as safe. We say, "I know these waters like the back of my hand." But what we mean is, we know these waters when they are still and when our boats are sound and when the sun

---

[2] Michelangelo, Marble statue, Galleria dell'Accademia, Florence, Italy, 1501-04

[3] Auguste Rodin, *The Thinker*, Rodin Museum, Paris, France, 1904

[4] Actually, August Rodin has told us what is on the Thinker's mind. *The Thinker* was created to be the capstone of a massive bronze sculpture called The Gates of Hell. The Thinker is Dante, and he is thinking about his epic poem *The Inferno*. Dante sits atop two massive doors—the gates of hell—and he is surrounded by tortured souls being taken into their eternal punishment. *The Thinker* is bent over with the burden of hell.

[5] Peter Paul Rubens, *The Lamentation Over the Dead Christ*, Oil on panel. 138cm × 178 cm. Royal Museum of Fine Arts Antwerp, circa 1618

is out and when our supplies are in order. And that, as it turns out, has nothing to do with actually knowing what churns in the depths or what gathers in the heavens. When the storm breaks out, we have much to learn.

For the men in the boat with Rembrandt, this storm was not their first encounter with their mortality. Early in Jesus's ministry, he and his disciples came to a town called Nain in the foothills of Mt. Tabor southeast of Nazareth.[6] As they drew near to the village, they heard the unmistakable cries of mourning coming from just inside the gate. This community's tragedy, whatever it was, was recent and the wounds were fresh.

The disciples watched as mourners trickled out like tears from the town's gate. Behind the mourners came four men carrying a dead man on a stretcher. The dead man's mother followed behind, weeping.

The disciples looked for the dead man's father or brothers. There were none. People from the procession said his mother was a widow and this was her only son. A loss like this meant the widow would have no one to care for her in her old age. Those who knew her situation all felt the same sting. No mother should have to bury her own child.

In those days people looked to their religious leaders to make sense of death and the grief it caused. But when Jesus's disciples looked at their teacher, they didn't see a man composing a speech. Instead, they saw a man dealing with his own grief. Jesus watched the dead son's mother weeping into her hands. He walked over and stood in front of her until she regarded him.

"Do not weep," he said.

His words were tender, but words alone would not stop these tears. They both knew this. Still, Jesus interrupted her mourning long enough for her to look up and see his compassion for her.

Jesus went over to the funeral bier and touched the pall.

The bearers stopped. In fact, in that moment, everything seemed to stop. When Jesus touched the board bearing the dead man, several people gasped because touching the dead defiled a rabbi's ceremonial purity. What

[6] Luke 7:11 17

was he thinking? Had he sunk so deep into his own empathy that he had forgotten himself?

Jesus whispered, "Young man."

The dead man's mother's sorrow changed to confusion. Did the rabbi just whisper something to her son?

Jesus said, "Young man, listen to my voice. Get up."

A huge gasp came from the stretcher as the body jerked like someone startled awake by a clap of thunder. The young man sat up and asked why he was on that board and why everyone looked so terrified.

Jesus helped him down and returned him to his mother. Fear seized the crowd of mourners. They weren't sure how to feel. Some wept even more. Others laughed in disbelief. One said what they were all feeling: "God has visited his people and he has given us a great prophet. Jesus of Nazareth speaks and the dead live again."

The disciples were no strangers to matters of mortality, but the ways Jesus responded to it were unlike anything they, or the rest of the world had ever seen. Reports of that miracle spread all around Judea and the surrounding countryside. Great crowds flocked to Jesus. As those crowds continued to grow, Jesus stayed on the move to manage them the best he could.

It was a world with no shortage of need, and people continued to brings theirs to him in droves. After one particularly intense day of ministry by the Sea of Galilee, Jesus asked his disciples to set off in a boat to get some peace and quiet. Weary, Jesus went to the bow of the boat and lay down. Rocking in the gentle swells of the sea, he fell asleep.

He awoke to a dripping, desperate face inches from his own shouting over the noise of a sudden storm, "Wake up! Don't you care that we are perishing?"[7]

A canyon wind had whipped the lake into such a torrent that the waves were beginning to break over the sides of the boat. She was sinking. Most of the souls on board were experienced seafarers, and all of them, in fact,

[7] Mark 4:38

except Jesus were working furiously to keep their boat adrift and so also their lives.

"Jesus, we're dying! Don't you care?" screamed Peter.

It was such an ironic question. The reason Jesus and his disciples were in the boat in the first place was to escape the crowds who continually pressed in around Jesus because he had come to be known as a healer who could raise the dead.[8] The masses sought him because he not only cared about their perishing, he stopped it. He even *reversed* it.

But there in the boat, paralyzed on a leprous-white sea, they knew this could only end in one of two ways: in death or in a miracle. In spite of their best efforts, they were headed for death and they were desperate. Did Jesus have anything for them like he had for the widow from Nain's son? Even if it was only words, they needed something.

THE MASTER

The Storm on the Sea of Galilee[9], Rembrandt Harmenszoon van Rijn's (1606-1669) only known seascape, is one of his most dramatic paintings, capturing that moment just after the disciples knew they would die if Jesus didn't save them and just before he did.

The five foot by four foot canvas hung in the Dutch Room on the second floor of the Isabella Stewart Gardner Museum for close to one hundred years. Everyone who looked at it saw the same thing; Rembrandt looking out through the frame to us—looking us dead in the eye. The terror on his face asked us what the disciples were asking Jesus: "Don't you care that we're perishing here?"

Rembrandt, who was known even to his own contemporaries as "The Master," was as much a storyteller as he was a painter. He cared about the

---

[8] Mark 1:29–2:12

[9] Rembrandt Harmenszoon van Rijn, *Storm on the Sea of Galilee*. Oil on Canvas, 160cm x 128cm, 1633

narratives behind his paintings, and painted them to tell as much of the story as he could in a single frame. One way he did this was by painting himself into several ubiquitous Biblical scenes. He did this not for vanity but for the sake of the story. He wanted to draw us in, capture our imaginations, instruct us on how we should relate to what was happening on the canvas, and bear witness to what he believed to be true about the world he painted and his place in it.

For example, in *The Raising of the Cross*[10], Rembrandt strains with three other men to lift the cross of Jesus into its base on Golgotha. He and Jesus are the only two men not draped in shadow. The contrast between them is stark. Jesus is naked, pale, and bloody; Rembrandt is wearing a rich man's clean, blue robe and matching beret. Rembrandt wants us to know that while he believed all people had a hand in Jesus' crucifixion (as seen in the array of soldiers, peasants, politicians, and faceless figures hidden in the background), as far as he is concerned, the one whose guilt shines brightest in that affair is his own.

In his painting, *The Prodigal Son in the Tavern*[11], Rembrandt is the glassy-eyed, drunk younger brother looking at us over his left shoulder as he holds a pint in one hand and a woman in the other. The woman in the painting is his wife, Saskia. By painting himself into this scene, Rembrandt confesses his great capacity for folly as well as his imminent need for mercy. We look on with a mix of pity and compassion. We know what the man in the story has squandered and what he has left behind. We know how his world is about to crumble. But we also know that his father loves him and is probably scanning the horizon for the young man's return even at that very moment. And we know the prodigal will return to his father's love, but not before he breaks.

By painting himself into the boat in *The Storm on the Sea of Galilee*, Rembrandt wants us to know that he believes his life will either be lost

---

[10] Rembrandt Harmenszoon van Rijn, *The Raising of the Cross*. Oil on Canvas, 95.7cm x 72.2cm, 1633

[11] Rembrandt Harmenszoon van Rijn, *The Prodigal Son in the Tavern*. Oil on canvas, 161cm x 131cm, 1635

in a sea of chaos or preserved by the Son of God. Those are his only two options. And by peering through the storm and out of the frame to us, he asks if we are not in the same boat.

THE COLLECTOR

America's first great art collector, Isabella Stewart Gardner (1840-1924), came to know this perishing all too well when her two-year-old son died in 1865. Heartbroken, she and her husband Jack began traveling the world in an effort to assuage their grief. Both Jack and Isabella came from wealthy families, so they were never wanting financially. This freed them to venture as far and wide as they pleased. And that they did. In their travels they began to collect art, both folk and fine, from around the globe.

Though their grief over the loss of their son eventually subsided, their appetite for art did not. In 1890, after twenty-five years of gathering, they realized they had assembled the makings of a world-class permanent collection of fine art that any museum would have been eager to call their own. So they set the folk art aside and focused on obtaining works from many of the world's greatest artists—Botticelli, Titian, Raphael, Manet, Degas, Vermeer, and Rembrandt. Their collection, Isabella said, "ought to have only a few, and all of them A number-ones."[12]

Before long, Isabella and Jack's collection grew so large that she felt it would be improper to keep it to themselves. She wanted to create a permanent home for their art—"a museum for the education and enjoyment of the public forever."[13] She and Jack purchased a plot of land in Boston's Fenway neighborhood and began to dream.

---

[12] From a letter from Isabella to her art dealer and friend, Bernard Bearenson, August 18, 1896

[13] From Isabella Stewart Gardner's last will and testament

Then in 1898 tragedy struck again. Jack died. Once again Isabella was thrown into grief, and as she had done when she lost her son, she turned to art to lead her through. Only this time instead of gathering more art others had created, she wanted to make something of her own—her own masterpiece, *her* museum: Fenway Court.

Isabella poured herself into the project. She was not content to simply meet with her builders and pay her contractors. She designed every aspect of the museum herself. Her architect, William Sears, joked that on this particular job he was little more than a carpenter and mechanical engineer carrying out the true architect's vision. Isabella designed an Italian renaissance Palazzo with great halls framing a grand courtyard in the center, just like the ones in Venice she and Jack used to stay in when they were younger and had the world by the tail.

Over the next few years, the four-story Fenway Court rose from the marshlands as one of the finer things many of its neighbors had ever seen. Once the structure was completed in 1902, Isabella then spent an entire year working on the interior design. Unimpressed with traditional gallery style museums, which, to her, were boring, bare rooms with pictures hanging on the walls, she arranged her collection to overwhelm her guests with the sense that they were getting a truly intimate experience with some of the world's most magnificent creations.

Each room would be its own living diorama featuring paintings, tapestries, furniture, and sculptures all arranged to immerse the patron in the experience of a culture and era they would never be able find anywhere other than her museum. "Love of art, not knowledge about the history of art, was her aim," the museum's brochure explained.

From the pieces in her collection to where she placed them in the palazzo to the architecture to the furniture to the floor plan, Fenway Court was just as Isabella wanted it. She was adamant that it remain that way, so much so that in her last will and testament she stipulated that if any changes were made to her collection after her death—if future trustees allowed anything to either be brought in or taken out—the entire collection would have to be turned over to Harvard for liquidation. Adding anything her collection would be like adding length to the Mona Lisa's hair, just as removing anything would be tantamount to cutting it.

Isabella Stewart Gardner, a woman of sorrows and acquainted with grief, wanted to bring something into this world that would not perish. She chose art. At the time of her death in 1924, Isabella had accumulated more than 2,500 tapestries, manuscripts, rare books, sculptures, pieces of furniture, and masterworks from Titian, Vermeer, Flinck, Michelangelo, Raphael, Whistler, Degas, Manet, Sargent, Botticelli, and the Dutch master himself, Rembrandt. She had given them a home. More than that, she had given them places of honor to be savored by the "rapt glad faces of those who love art."[14]

When asked why she was so protective of keeping Fenway Court just as she had made it, the widow who buried her son all those years earlier said, "My museum will live."[15]

THE TAKE

The sensors on the security door revealed that the thieves had to make two trips.

The thirteen stolen works included Johannes Vermeer's *The Concert*[16] (one of only 35 confirmed Vermeers in existence), a Flinck landscape, a three thousand year old Chinese vase from the Shang Dynasty, one Manet, five Degas, and three Rembrandts—one, a postage stamp sized self-portrait etching; one, his formal *Lady and Gentleman in Black*;[17] and last, one

---

[14] From John Updike's poem, *Stolen*, 2000

[15] From the documentary film, *Stolen*. Flourish Films, 2008

[16] Johannes Vermeer, *The Concert*, Oil on canvas, 72.5 cm × 64.7 cm, circa 1664. Whereabouts unknown.

[17] Rembrandt Harmenszoon van Rijn, *A Lady and Gentleman in Black*, oil on canvas, 131.6cm x 109cm, 1633. Whereabouts unknown.

of the Museum's most prominently displayed works, *The Storm on the Sea of Galilee.*

Together, the thirteen stolen pieces of art amounted to the largest property theft in America's history with an estimated value of more than $500 million.

The most valuable works were taken from the museum's Dutch Room on the second floor. "Strong personalities dominate this room," the museum guide says. "Looking down from the walls are a queen, a doctor, an archduchess, a lawyer, an artist, and an art collector."[18] Even in the elite company of Isabella's other Dutch and Flemish masterpieces, there was no disputing that Rembrandt's *The Storm on the Sea of Galilee* ruled the room.

Rembrandt painted *The Storm on the Sea of Galilee* in 1633, shortly after moving from his home in Leiden to Amsterdam. He wanted to establish himself as one of the city's masters of Biblical and geo-political portraiture and historical scenes. Rembrandt's fine brushwork and bright palette were characteristic of his early style, which featured detail as intricate as the braid of a rope or the crow's feet around a man's eyes.

Rembrandt's "ability not only to represent a sacred history, but also to seize our attention and immerse us in an unfolding pictorial drama"[19] makes the *The Storm on the Sea of Galilee* transcend the scene itself. The story here is about so much more than one group of men getting caught up in that one storm on that one afternoon. This painting is about all of us. Rembrandt retraces the old story that pits man against nature as the angry sea tosses that fully rigged boat with her terrified passengers around like a toy. And he pits the vulgar against the divine as one disciple vomits over the leeward rail while another, only two feet away, holds on to the Second Person of the Blessed Trinity, pleading for him to save them.

---

[18] Excerpted from the Isabella Steward Gardner Museum visitor guide
[19] Michael Zell, *Christ in the Storm on the Sea of Galilee, Eye of the Beholder,* edited by Alan Chong et al. (Boston: ISGM and Beacon Press, 2003): p. 143.

The crime scene revealed that while the thieves had plenty of time to handle the art with care, they chose not to. One Rembrandt was left behind, bent and scuffed on the floor. Vermeer's *The Concert* had been knocked out of its frame, as had Manet's *Chez Tortoni*.[20] (In what could only be seen as an act of mockery, the thieves left Manet's empty frame in a chair in the security supervisor's office.)

Rembrandt's *The Storm on the Sea of Galilee* fared even worse. Rather than risk getting caught with the five-foot canvas, the thieves took a knife and cut the painting out of its stretcher boards. The frame, complete with its tiny brass plaque at the bottom, which read, simply, "Rembrandt," was left hanging empty on the wall.

THE MARKET

Anthony Amore, the Gardner Museum's security director said, "Art is not stolen by master criminals, but by common criminals [...] It is less like *The Thomas Crown Affair* and more like a Cohen Brothers movie."[21]

Art thieves are rarely art collectors. Collectors want to show others what they have. Criminals want to keep their cache hidden and turn it into money as soon as possible. Because art thieves are not often collectors, they don't always know what they are taking. In 2003, one thief made off with DaVinci's *Madonna with the Yarn Winder*,[22] not realizing he had stolen one of the most famous and valuable paintings in the world. When he tried to sell it no one would touch it because it was too famous.[23]

---

[20] Édouard Manet, *Chez Tortoni*, Oil on canvas, 26cm x 34cm, ca. 1878–1880. Whereabouts unknown. [21] Matt Lebovic, "Is the Hunt for Rembrandt's stolen 'Galilee' Almost Over?," *The Times of Israel*, October 3, 2013

[22] Leonardo da Vinci, *Madonna with the Yarn Winder*, Oil on canvas, 50.2cm x 36.4cm, c.1510. Private collection

[23] *What Happens to Stolen Art?* BBC News, August 23, 2004

Stolen art is a burden few can manage. What can a thief do with half a billion in stolen art when the paintings taken in the heist are featured in every newspaper, magazine, and news show around the world? The average law-abiding citizen gets stuck on this question because they assume the point is for the thief to try to get something close to what the art is worth. A one hundred million dollar stolen Vermeer, even at a discount, should fetch the thief fifty million dollars, right?

Wrong. Thieves in possession of well known works of art—Vermeer's, Rembrandt's, Monet's, DaVinci's—know that attempting to sell the art outright almost guarantees their arrest.

So what happens to art once it is taken? Typically, a stolen piece of art meets one of four fates: it is either destroyed, held for ransom, used as a black market currency, or sold as a high quality replica of itself.

Of course, there are instances where thieves steal art because they want to keep it for themselves, but that seldom turns out well. Stephane Breitwieser, a 32-year-old waiter who lived with his mother in eastern France, stole hundreds of pieces of art from museums in Germany, Switzerland, and France. He stole them because he liked them; he displayed them in his mother's home. When he was arrested for stealing a bugle, of all things, his mother, in an effort to hide his crimes, burned many of the pieces in his collection. At the time of Breitwieser's arrest, he had gathered close to two billion dollars in stolen art.[24]

Investigators estimate that 20% of all stolen art meets a similar fate. The stress and inconvenience of holding such precious public treasures ends up being more than the thieves bargained for. With nowhere to turn and no way to give it back, they destroy their prize.

The FBI says only 5% of the world's stolen art is ever recovered. Often, these pieces were stolen for the purpose of returning them for a ransom. This art tends to end up back on the museum wall. For some thieves, this is the plan all along—steal a painting, cut out letters from a

---

[24] Robert Poole, "Ripped from the Walls (and the Headlines)," *Smithsonian Magazine*, July 2005

newspaper and glue them together into a ransom note, and hope for the best.

For others, they're after a ransom of a different kind. Some criminals have the foresight to know that due to their unlawful lifestyle, they will likely one day be arrested for something. This is a question of when, not if. Facilitating the return of a stolen treasure becomes a strategic bargaining chip when they go to plead down their charges. Criminals know that law enforcement agencies look great in the public eye when they recover stolen art, and there is no such thing as too much goodwill between these agencies and the communities they serve.

This leaves approximately 75% of the world's stolen art simply unaccounted for—in the wind. Once the Gardner art trundled away from the museum in the back of a panel van, it took on a completely new purpose. It ceased to exist "for the education and enjoyment of the public forever"[25] and most likely became a form of currency. Black market paintings and sculptures end up traveling the world like a twenty-dollar bill or a pawned watch.

How does this work? Suppose someone drives off with a Monet worth $10,000,000. That painting might be traded right away for $1,000,000 worth of high quality cocaine. The cocaine dealer then sits on the painting for a year while the buzz around it dies down. Then he trades it to an arms dealer for a cache of weapons for his cartel. Another year passes and the arms dealer trades the Monet to a weapons supplier who knows a black market art dealer. Now the painting has been off the grid for a few years and is five people removed from the thief and his crime without one dollar actually exchanging hands. The black market has laundered the painting and the memory of its theft to a point where it can begin to appear in unscrupulous deals and move from private sale to private sale for years, even decades, before ever emerging on the open market or being discovered an attic at some estate sale.

---

[25] From Isabella Stewart Gardner's last will and testament

Stolen art fetches roughly 10% of its actual value in that first sale. But the further it travels from the crime, the greater the buyer's plausible deniability and thus the safer the purchase and the higher the price tag. The laws surrounding art theft don't exactly deter thieves. They know how the system works.

In the US, the National Stolen Property Act protects collectors from going jail for owning stolen art unless it can be proven that they knew they were buying stolen merchandise, which is almost impossible to demonstrate with laundered art since one of the hallmarks of the black market is secrecy. In the Netherlands, the law says that after 20 years, a piece of stolen art becomes the legal property of whoever possesses it.

In 2004 six men stole Edvard Munch's *The Scream*[26] (worth more than $100,000,000) from a museum wall in Oslo. They were arrested, but only three were convicted, and only two served any jail time; one man got six years and the other got four. Stephane Breitwieser, the French waiter, spent just four years in jail for stealing close to two billion dollars worth of art.

One former art thief said in an interview that criminals know if they steal a Rembrandt they might get three to five years, but if they steal the equivalent of what that Rembrandt is worth in cash or commodities, they might face 25 years to life.[27] Stolen art has long been prized as a low-risk, high reward currency for funding criminal activity.

If those pieces of the Gardner art haven't been destroyed, or held for ransom, or passed around like a briefcase full of cash, they likely fall into one other grim scenario. They have been sold as high quality replicas of themselves.

How does this work? Say, for example, a thief steals a lesser-known Rembrandt. Rembrandt had many pupils over the years—young painters who studied in his studio alongside the Master himself. These students

---

[26] Edvard Munch, *The Scream*, Oil, tempera, and pastel on cardboard, 91cm × 73.5cm, National Gallery, Oslo, Norway, 1893

[27] Cornelius Poppe, "Seven Questions: A Reformed Stolen-Art Dealer Tells All," *Foreign Policy Magazine*, February 20, 2008

learned to mimic Rembrandt's technique and style. Many of his protégés became so skilled in the art of imitation that historians have been debating the authenticity of hundreds of canvases and etchings attributed to him. German art historian Wilhelm von Bode quipped, "Rembrandt painted 700 pictures. Of these, 3,000 are still in existence."

A savvy con man with a gullible target could convince his potential buyer that the painting he has to sell came from one of Rembrandt's own students. All he needs to do to make his case is turn to the painting itself. The detail in this unknown artist's copy would have required unobstructed access to the original. See how the light hits the woman's nose in the exact way Rembrandt painted it. Look at the tassels on the man's coat. Take a sample of the paint to a lab if you like. You will discover it is, in fact, paint from the 17th century—Dutch in origin. It may not be a true Rembrandt, the con explains, but it comes from the brush of the Master's protégé. The palette, the scale, the detail, and even the signature all say that this is a rare work in its own right—easily worth a percentage of the masterwork it apes. For a mere $100,000, you could own an actual 17th century painting from Rembrandt's studio. Perhaps it was even painted on the same easel that held the original. Chances are it was.

This has to be the most insidious option of the four. Rather than reduce a work of art to ash, the thief burns it from our memory. Rather than holding it for a ransom worthy of its pedigree, it endures the indignity of being sold for a pittance. Rather than circulate the painting among art lovers, corrupt though they may be, the thief removes the painting from circulation and banishes it to a fate worse than fire—a life of obscurity where it continues to exist in a world that will never find it. Its new owner doesn't know it is real and the seller is praying he never finds out.

Rembrandt's *The Storm on the Sea of Galilee* has been in the wind for close to twenty-five years now. There is a $5,000,000 reward for the recovery of the Gardner art. So far no one has stepped forward to claim that reward. There have been no arrests. No demands for ransom. No legitimate sightings. Despite thousands of tips, leads, and suspects shared between the

FBI, the US Attorney's office in Massachusetts, local, federal, and international law enforcement, no one knows who stole the art or where it is.

Ron Gollobin, a Boston crime beat reporter, said, "There's a five million dollar reward. That's a pretty powerful statement. Absolute silence. Not one peep as to who might have done this."[28] While it may be in the possession of someone who is simply biding their time, the silence suggests the sober probability that we have seen the last of *The Storm on the Sea of Galilee*.

Still, every year on the anniversary of the theft, the Gardner Museum issues a press release asking for its return. In the release, like the parent of a kidnapped child going on television to describe how to properly use an EpiPen, the museum explains that the missing art should be kept at 68 degrees Fahrenheit with 50 percent humidity.

THE FRAME

The Dutch Room's brownish gray fleur-de-lis wall covering now fills Rembrandt's frame like an eerie calm after a violent storm. Aside from perhaps a few canvas fibers and paint chips from the 17th century embedded the cracks of the museum floor, there remains no sign of Rembrandt's boat or any of the souls on board. All are lost.

Museum-goers visit the Dutch Room like mourners passing the grave of a loved one. They describe Rembrandt's empty frame as "an unholy tragedy, a monstrous corruption of beauty."[29] Some refuse to even set foot in the room. Those who know how that museum came to be are offended by the theft—not because of how much the stolen art was worth, but because what the thieves did was rude. It was disrespectful of Isabella's gift and inconsiderate of her grief.

---

[28] From the documentary film, *Stolen*. Flourish Films, 2008
[29] Milton Esterow, "Inside the Gardner Case," *ARTNews*, May 1, 2009

Isabella Stewart Gardner walked in the way of the widow from Nain and had carried her sorrows to this place in the hope of finding some rest. When she lost her baby in a sea of grief, she turned to beauty for healing. When she lost her husband, she determined to create something that would not die—a museum that would live forever. And she would give it to the world.

Isabella was one person in a long line of many who have, in their own way, tried to arrest the decay of a dying creation. She wanted to give us something beautiful, something lasting, something whole born out of a groaning too deep for words.[30] It was a defiant act of war against death using beauty as her weapon.

Whoever cut *The Storm on the Sea of Galilee* from its frame did so with Rembrandt looking straight at him. Did the two men make eye contact? Did the man disguised as a Boston police officer understand what Rembrandt was trying say?

Listen. This is a hard world. It is a world where children die and where widows grieve. This is the nature of the storm we are all painted into. The same sea that lures us in with its beauty and bounty surges with a power that can destroy us without warning. And eventually there comes a reckoning. Rembrandt knew this well. So did Isabella Stewart Gardner. So did every man in the boat.

Has the thief learned this yet? Or is he still glassy-eyed at the tavern bar in a distant country, unaware that he has now painted himself into Isabella's storm. His workmanship now hangs in Rembrandt's place, leaving behind a frame that has become something like the location of a dead drop, a place where messages are exchanged between people who are not meant to see each other.

The empty frame is a note from the thief that tells Isabella that though she may want to create something beyond the reach of death, that is not

---

[30] Romans 8:26

something this world affords. She can dress up the pain all she likes, but nothing she has made will last forever. This is a world where thieves break in and steal.[31] It is a place where beautiful things are destroyed, where precious treasures are sold for a pittance, where talents are buried in the ground never to be seen again. This is a world where we are constantly trying to tell each other that we are not what we truly are. The gloom of criminality enshrouds us. The thief knew this well. So did Rembrandt. So did every man in the boat.

Does Isabella?

Things will not always be this way. Sad things such as these will one day come untrue. The Apostle Paul said those who put their faith in Jesus are like earthen vessels with glory inside—frames that hold masterpieces. He said, "We are afflicted in every way, but not crushed; perplexed, but not driven to despair; persecuted, but not forsaken; struck down, but not destroyed; always carrying in the body the death of Jesus, so that the life of Jesus may also be manifested in our bodies… So we do not lose heart. Though our outer self is wasting away, our inner self is being renewed day by day. For this light momentary affliction is preparing for us an eternal weight of glory beyond all comparison."[32]

The disciple's question reverberates down through the ages—does God care about our perishing? Jesus came treading upon our roughest seas, speaking peace into the gale. And he will do it again. His triumph over the grave calls those who are perishing to be born again into a new and living hope. The peace he has brought by his resurrection is neither myth nor fantasy. It is an inheritance that will never perish, kept for those who believe, world without end.[33]

His is a kingdom that will live. But it is the only one of its kind.

If *The Storm on the Sea of Galilee* still exists, Rembrandt, in all his glory, is tucked away in some closet, attic, or vault, hidden from the world.

---

[31] Matthew 6:19–24

[32] 2 Corinthians 4:7–10, 16–18 (ESV)

[33] 1 Peter 1:3

He is still clutching that rope; still trying to keep his hat from flying off his head. And he is looking out into our world for anyone who will make eye contact. If he still exists, it is quite a storm he is caught in.

Someday soon, if the Bible is true, Jesus will stand and say to widows and thieves alike, "Peace, be still." His words will be followed by an unprecedented, eternal calm.[34]

Knowing this helps us now. Whatever we suffer, we need not grieve as those who have no hope.

So we learn to hope in a coming kingdom. But we do so knowing that in this one, at least for now, Rembrandt is in the wind.

---

[34] Revelation 21:1–5

Fact: It's in Russ Ramsey's closet.

WHEN I SEE IT
by Jen Rose Yokel

I know poetry when I see it.
It dances and sings and leaps
across the page.
It shapes the white space
breathing life into ink marks and wood pulp.

I know poetry when I see it—
The essence of truth compressed
into a line so small, yet so full.
You read it over and over again
To know it by heart.
You write it down word for word,
letter for letter,
period for period,
for the wonder of what it felt like
to write it.

I know poetry when I see it—
standing on my toes

straining for a glimpse
over the shoulders of giants,
feeling small and speechless
in their presence.

And sometimes—

I feel the surge of words
begging to be set loose.
I hear them whispering
between the notes of a song,
or in the voice of a friend,
or in a flare of epiphany.

I doubt their worth and wonder if they matter,
and if they could mean anything
to anyone
but me.

But I write them
(or at least I try to)
to honor in the smallest way
the poetry I've seen.

Like a little girl
in her mother's heels
five sizes too large.

AT A LOSS FOR WORDS
by Eric Peters

W hen I am asked why, for the first time in my middle age, I picked up paint and brush with an eye toward creative expression, I say it was because I needed to learn to be brave. Melodrama aside, it was not that I was afraid of painting, it was that I was afraid of *failing* at the act, and fear of failure has everything to do with summoning courage.

Until that moment in early 2010, I had ventured nowhere near a blank canvas since Ms. Vollenweider's seventh-grade art class. With her perpetually rumpled hair, Ms. V. was a bright soul, and I can still hear her cigarette-raspy "That is *WONderful*!" reverberating off the metal blinds of her McKinley Junior High classroom. Wandering the aisles between desks, looking over our shoulders and offering tutelage and insight, she said the same thing about nearly all of her student's projects, no matter their quality: *WONderful*. To my knowledge, none of us were child prodigies, and I doubt anything we ever created in her classroom was actually all that wonderful, but we were, I am certain, buoyed by her graceful comments. The fact that I can still hear her saying those words is proof that words are not lost for long.

But at no point between middle school and middle age did I attempt to paint anything except the exterior of my house. From time to time I had a mind to exercise the artful side of my brain in that medium, but, invariably,

I convinced myself that any such attempt would be a long, long way from *WONderful*. So like a good boy, I dismissed the thought, insisting on song-writing and words rather than shapes and colors.

For years, I've marveled at the wizardry of Van Gogh's starry nights, his golden Arlesian skies, the manic crows erupting from fields, the oblong furniture sitting out of perspective inside his oblong room, the sad and weary faces of his ordinary subjects. They spoke in their own wordless ways. And recently I've come to admire the remarkable, though abstract, works of artists like Mark Rothko, Arthur Dove, and Charles Burchfield. Theirs are works unbounded by conformity or convention. Looking at the world from different, unexpected angles, they were willing to construct scenes they themselves wanted to see, free of any language requiring words. Though I could appreciate their works, I inevitably situated myself on the outside looking in: a spectator. There is a time for spectating, but to will-fully snuff out a recurring inclination is not only futile, but ignorant. I eventually came to realize that, ironically, what prevented me from trying my hand and imagination at brush and palette was my active imagination itself—the very trait that fuels the art and the act. Over and over again, I was convinced I would fail. *Why bother? You will only make a mess of it.* So I never tried.

I suppose the same goes for all our imagining and dreaming. From birth we face up to an adult world. Given no choice but to cleanse ourselves of childhood, we are expected to mature into conforming, civil adults who aspire to the zenith of a nine-to-five job, impressive portfolio, plush retire-ment fund, and all the while keeping secrets a secret. Fears, insecurities, and perhaps a road-block of words themselves, crowd the path until we find ourselves no longer scaling a molehill, but clinging, white-knuckled, to the sheer face of a cloud-piercing mountain. It is there, breathless, confused, and overwhelmed, that we ultimately ask ourselves, if we can summon the words: "*Why bother?*"

I paint for this reason: brushstrokes and impasto daubs of pthalo blue do not involve words. And, being often at a loss for them, that has made all the difference. The act of painting certainly involves a language, but having made a career of lyric and melody—valuing both—I reached the point in my middle-age where I needed a creative outlet (painting) for my occupational creative outlet (songwriting), a mode of expression that might grant me the opportunity to "speak" without saying a single word—private grunts, humming, and swears notwithstanding. Had I not found such a means of expression, the mountain and the path might very well have cracked and crumbled, taking me down with it. To avoid falling, I had to *choose* to try my hand at an alternate form of expression, regardless of fear, failure, and daunting crags. I didn't need to be noteworthy. I didn't have to be good at all. I only needed to try it, to pursue authenticity. I had to *move*, to allow myself the freedom to do so, to not allow myself to be bullied by fear and paralysis.

I don't dislike words. Having made a career of them, I place great value on them. It's only that I get tired of having to use them. But man shall not live by bread—or words—alone. Words, as everyone knows, are powerful. To contradict the inviolable childhood adage, words can and do indeed hurt. Alternately, a few well-chosen words can be sparks in big dark places, veritable safety ledges along sheer mountainsides. *WONderful.* Words are necessary, but words are, at times, better left unspoken. A devoted introvert, I find myself fatigued by having to speak, by having to hear myself talk. It is entirely possible that I idolize silence and solitude, and if there be any sin in such valuation, I am surely doomed. Truthfully, there are moments I wish to be left alone, to not only relieve my varying hyperacusis and downright moodiness, but to also reacquire cosmos in the midst of chaos.

The fearful, dark, chaotic streaks coexist alongside the palette's lighter fare. Hues and shades contrast, invading one another's spaces as plumes of color meander their way through the darks and monotones. One can scarcely exist without the other, much in the same way a song lyric delivered without melody falls flat and hollow. Strokes of brilliant light outline the sanity of living, exposing the hidden ridges, revealing the windward and lee sides, darkness doing everything it can to quell the courage hiding among the clefts of our imagination. No longer children, we still look "up" at our world out of awe, fear, and perhaps hope, but we are not without the tools necessary to summon courage when silence is the sky's only trait. The glimmering sky blesses the fields, and the fields return the favor. I, in my renderings, can only hope to be a similar blessing, even when—especially when—I am at a loss for words.

SOMETHING NEW

Words by Jen Rose Yokel
Visuals by Jonny Jimison

I used to think poems
were found under rocks,
hiding in the dew-drenched
dirt of the forest.

When you fell into a trance
or stirred up the right mood,
they came in some
mystical revelation.

the words would descend

like a thousand  perfect raindrops

and puddle together in brilliance.

—just as I hit
that moment of zen,

the overfull calender
keeps me running,

so many great lines
evaporating at red lights,

Where is the art in this?

Or maybe they are
tumbling in an everyday ocean,
rocks weathered smooth,
washed up
on a word-covered coastline,

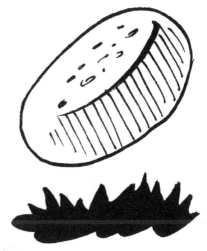

Waiting for hands to
turn them over

and over

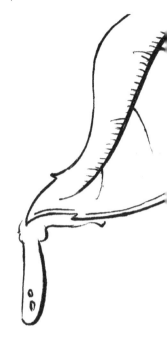

seeking

something

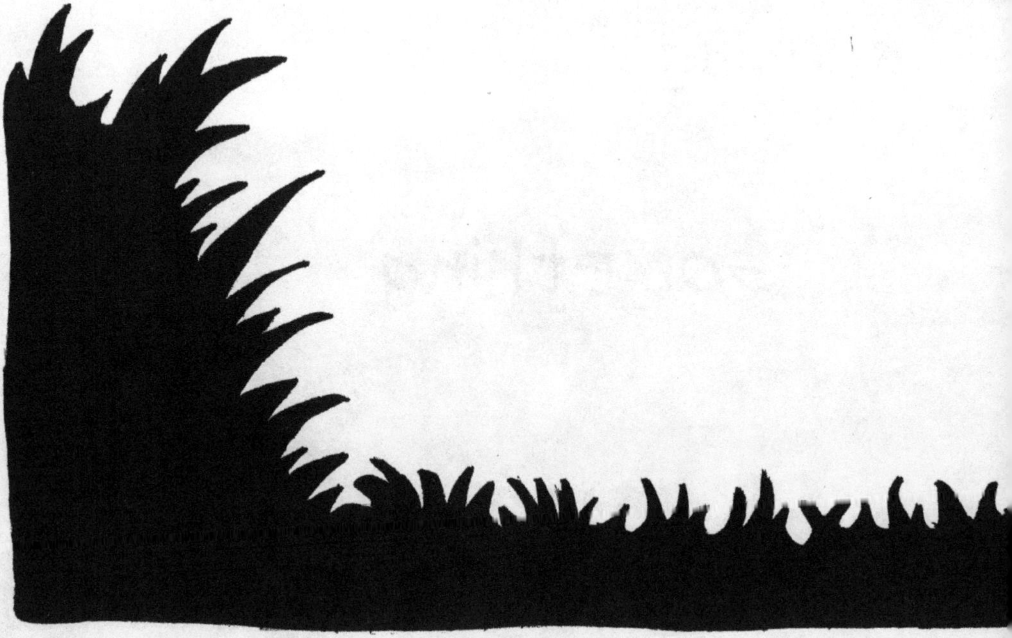

new.

Fact: Eric Peters once wrestled a giraffe to the ground and taught it to call him "Pappy."

THE POET
by Chris Yokel

A poet is not a master of words,
he cannot make them come and go,
he cannot conjure them with a wand,
he cannot cull them from a cauldron,
nor gain them in a devil's bargain.

He is a kite waiting for the wind
to bear him upward into the heights.

If he has any skill at all,
it is in the patience of waiting,
the stillness of listening,
and the readiness to act.

First Fact: The original name of Tiberius Creache, villain of *The Fiddler's Gun,* was "Philibottomus Munche."
Second Fact: A good writer listens to his editor.

PROVIDENCE ATHENAEUM
by Chris Yokel

I have so many sounds
pounding away at my skull,
but today I will listen
to the slow breathing of old books
as their ponderance of thought
strains the shelves.
I will apologize to this wooden chair
as it creaks and complains
under my weight.
My mind will spread its arms,
stretch, yawn, unfold
as the chitter of librarians
flutters between the shelves,
and the severe eyes
of Shakespeare,
Dante,
and Milton
shrink me down to a grade-school boy,

tongue out,
feet tapping below my chair,
scrawling down my restless rhymes
with the rhythmic scratch
of a chewed-up pencil.

THE BLACK HORIZON (PART II)
Story and Illustrations by Jamin Still

FOUNDATIONS

How high are we building it?" asked Sesha. She was out of breath and the way she flexed her fingers seemed to indicate that her hands hurt from carrying the sharp rocks. She didn't complain, though. Sweat beaded on her forehead and ran down her cheeks.

Jacob looked back at the circle of stones he had laid. They were stacked atop one another like the stone walls that bordered the fields. The circle was only up to his knees. "We have a ways to go."

They worked in rhythm with the sound of the waves on the shore below until the sun neared the horizon.

"I have to be home soon," said the girl. "Are we finished?"

"No," said Jacob.

"What is it? It looks like a well."

Jacob lightly touched one of the stones and said, "It's a tower."

"Like The Hourglass?"

"I suppose so." He swallowed and looked away.

"What happened in there?" Sesha asked.

For a long time Jacob said nothing and only stared out at the horizon. Much had happened inside The Hourglass, but those injuries, those pains, the ones sustained inside the tower, had long since healed. He cleared his throat and said, "You've heard the stories."

"I would have waited for you, Jacob."

Jacob leaned down so that she wouldn't see his face and picked up another stone. He brushed it off and laid it carefully. Then another. Finally he said, "I think I'd like to work alone tomorrow."

SONGS FOR A DROWNING LAND
by Douglas McKelvey

Before 1948, Old Butler was a hamlet of more than six hundred people and fifty businesses tucked into the northeastern corner of Tennessee. By the end of 1948, it no longer existed.

By design of the Tennessee Valley Authority, the former town and all her farms and roads and countryside were swallowed by the waters of a newly formed lake, submerged for the greater good. It was the first drowned town I ever heard stories of, and it roosted in my imagination. I've since read that well over half the states in the US have their own similar histories. In the seven Southern states under TVA jurisdiction alone, it is estimated that 15,000 families (and 30,000 graves) were relocated before work was finished on the large-scale dam-building projects. Ghostly remnants of some of those old towns linger still beneath the surfaces of our lakes.

When one considers the histories of our drowned towns, one wonders about the sorts of losses that couldn't have been accounted for in the government ledgers. When one has wondered long enough, one might even begin to write poems about them.

THE SONG OF THE GIN-DRUNKARD

What I have lost is not money. The new house is better
than an even trade and I will abandon it anyway
come Spring. I tried to remind them at the last town
hall meeting how it was my grandfather laid

the red bricks in the courthouse square. Paving those streets
with a care that is nowadays hard to come by. You could
trace your fingers over those old seams for five days
straight and not find space so much as to wedge a fingernail.

Can you not—based on that lone mathematical fact—work back
wards to the kind of folk my people used to be? Clumped
here like thirsty birchwood trees, loam-fed beside a trickling stream,
their spacing thinned by Winters? What now, would all such hardships mean?

If you find even ten righteous men, will you still destroy this town? I spat against the
ground; some spinster hissed. Men seized me by the wrists and set me out. It's
true I was clouded by gin but it was not my own offense I gave vent to. It was
the cries of better men whose works we stood to shed like locust skins.

Perhaps I should have crawled back in to tell them then how his theology was
best expressed in the symmetry of his trade. How he made things slowly and
to last knowing the care to align each brick would be multiplied by ten thousand
footfalls it must bear up under, and give no cause for stumbling.

The Song of the Schoolmaster

The article's author claims evidence of Atlantis at some exotic
latitude; her old stones and pillars sunken to the seabed, tossed like dice
upon her settled foundations. His descriptions smell strongly of snake oil and

lecture halls; constructs built to agitate the sediment of imagination like a
crawfish scuttling for cover. Suckers will rush to reward him for the thrill of
false wonders. Still, I am not unsympathetic to his cause. I have studied the

expressions of a dozen schoolboys as they puzzled out place names in their
geography primers, their lips trying to fit over the ancient formations of words
as if their very tongues were in labor; as if speaking them were itself an act

of creation that could bring lost things back to life.

THE SONG OF THE CAVALRY SCOUT

I might stay here a while longer yet and let the waters fill. They say it will be
a slow baptism. Barefoot I can slosh through this house some days still, till my

mattress is seeped; my hearth sodden; my stores spoilt. I'm canny to keep the
snakes out. I will not be missed any more than I have already been. I had no

wife and gradually grew absent from the stove-side soirée forty years ago; it is a
younger crowd gathers at the mercantile now—men in their seventies. The

future is theirs. They will move on. My generation went to war and returned like
last thin trickles of blood, drying as we ran. We could only make it so far back

before we hardened. It's curious to consider what parts of us were left: one
finger and a thumb I relinquished at Russelville, mangled with the ruined ribs

of a good mare; our wounds oozing crimson as crushed rhubarb. We flew in a
dumb panic, flushing like quail a ring of rebels too shocked to raise their rifles

till we'd already passed—their trailing shots strayed wild overhead like a final
salute to the dying. I woke wounded against her cold husk and walked home to

farm—the plowhandle feeling like an alien thing; the sorghum strangely bitter. I opened a repair shop one year but closed it on account of customers wanting

conversation. When my roof wanted fixing, I allowed the rain entry, collecting it in cans. The sky pressed hard to the ground. I did not understand why progress

mattered. When the preacher knocked at the door, I no longer answered. The last time I sat for a shave, eager local boys dropped in for a trim, slapping backs

before they shipped off to France. One glanced rudely at my claw like a casualty viewed through the wrong end of a field glass. I paid the barber and passed

between them to retrieve my hat and couldn't think of a damn thing to say; as if the war I'd seen was a private thing I had carried home to plant in my own field:

A weed burr clinging to the pants leg.

THE SONG OF THE SURVEYOR'S ASSISTANT

We make lakes

to cleanse our valleys

of old ghosts

and scrub,

damming rivers

with a precision

engineered to

achieve un-chaos

measuring to

the last thin inch each

outcrop of rock

as if topography were

equal to mastery;

as if the land had not

wanted to drown

for good but experts had

known better.

Our boasts are feeble

as solstice light;

temporal as weathered

sandstone juts.

Our mastery is a

last dying of

echoes down ridge

lines at dusk

we make lakes

but there must

have been a time

now blind to us

when gods and

furious men damned

the whole world

to make deep

oceans rush.

The Song of the Adulterers

Watauga Dam was a judgment built slowly
and in our full view. Six years we visited the site
like sinners heckling Noah: the only
show in town. At first we came whenever
we could, spreading our blanket on far
hills, revelers at the world's end. How soon
the shadows of the structure—sundial-like—overstretched
that distance; how chill the pall

when whole rivers were stopped at last, when swirling
waters filled the hollows. We drove out the sleeping
child in secret to blink upon the bowl's rim, conspicuous
as spotted goats, bleating uncertainly while the lake
poured into what had always been our bedroom windows;
dark liquids filling the deep cavities we abandoned.

Fact: In another drowning land, Ulysses Everett McGill saw a cow on the roof of a cotton house and overcame many an obstacle in pursuit of great fortune. Also, Delmar thought Pete was a horny toad—though he was not.

THE FIRST ELEMENT
by Jen Rose Yokel

In the beginning
there was nothing,
yet your spirit moved
over the waters.

In the end of an age,
a flood purged the world.

In the beginning of another,
you in human mold
of earth and air came up
from the river, cleansed.

And your servant trembled
knowing his baptisms
could not cleanse one
already pure.

In the now,
I dare to wade into the ocean
that gives and takes,
that plays with children,
that wrecks men on rocks

A fluid force,
a tender tempest,
much like you.

LONELY IN VARBERG
by Andrew Peterson

An old fortress, staunch and windblown,
Rises from the sea at Varberg.
I think of the night my bride and I
Put on our coats, scarves, gloves,
And strolled the redoubts, piled with snow,
On a black night in March.
I loved her then, and I love her now,
And need her the same, a fortress,
A mercy immovable by wave or wind or winter.

But now she's an ocean away, in Tennessee,
Where the spring of mid-April
Has laid a garland of grass, dandelion,
And daffodil upon the hill where she waits.
Our spring chicks, she tells me, are losing
Their downy yellow feathers
And are rusty with adolescence;

The lettuce, spinach, broccoli, and kale
are standing taller in the longer light,
Readying themselves for harvest,
Joyful in their sustaining fate.

The bugs, too, have come awake,
Nuisances (ticks), vicious invaders
(mosquitoes), and winged flowers
(swallowtail butterflies), along with planets
Orbiting suns orbiting galaxies
(husbands, wives, children).

Merciful Father, bring me home,
To flesh and blood, bone and breath,
Because a memory of our warm love
On a cold night in Varberg castle
Is not enough—though I must admit,
It is better than a fabrication,
However tender I might
Imagine it. The green hills of home
Are as real as the memory that wakes
Me in these sleepy borderlands,
Where I live in memory, and home
Remembers me, I pray, by my absence.

We stare at each other from either shore.

MY FOUR VOWS
by Thomas McKenzie

S everal months ago, I was invited to a ceremony. A teenager from my church
was to be awarded the rank of Eagle Scout. I've known this guy since he
was tiny; he, his parents, and his brothers are dear to me. I was honored to be a
witness to this event.

The ceremony was well attended by the boy's family and friends, and by
the rest of his large Boy Scout troop. Toward the end, the scoutmaster invited
all the other Eagle Scouts in the room to come forward, to gather around
the boy in what was called "the eagle's nest." As an Eagle Scout myself, I was
happy to go forward. A few words were said, and then the scoutmaster asked
us to take an oath. He would say a phrase, and then we were to repeat it. This
went on for a minute or so. But while all the men around me were repeating
after the scoutmaster, I stood silently.

After the ceremony, refreshments were served. While eating a cookie, a
friend of the new Eagle Scout approached me. With no malice, but simply
with curiosity, she said, "I noticed that you didn't say the oath, and I'm wondering why not." I told her I had not intended to stick out, nor did I intend
to be offensive. However, I take my oaths, my promises and pledges, very
seriously. I had not been given the text of this oath in advance, so I had no

idea what I was being asked to pledge. Furthermore, as I listened, there were promises that I simply could not have made. My life is governed by my oaths; I can't take one frivolously.

There are four oaths which inform the whole of my life. They are oaths of baptism, marriage, ordination, and oblation. Together, these mark the boundaries of my existence, the barriers that keep me safe, focused, and (hopefully) at peace.

My first oath was taken for me by my parents and godparents. When I was a baby, at my baptism, they promised that I would renounce the devil, receive the Lordship of Christ, and follow after his ways. When I was old enough, I affirmed these promises at my confirmation. Since then, I have presented my own daughters for baptism, and I have baptized (or supported the baptism of) many other people.

My baptismal oath is my promise to follow and obey Jesus. This is my first and most important vow, and all my other promises hang on it. I am bound to Jesus by his faithfulness to me, and I have decided (and decide over and over again) to be faithful to him. A significant part of my faithfulness, by the way, is my repentance when I am not faithful.

Because I have made this vow, the question of lordship is settled. I do not ask "who is in charge?" I know who rules, and I know on whom I can depend. Furthermore, I know upon whom my children and my church depend. My promises at their baptisms focus me on the centrality of Jesus in my daily life.

My second oath is my promise to love my wife with true fidelity. This vow I made to her and to God in the presence of Christ's church. I am bound to my wife in a way that I cannot be to any other person. She is my primary human relationship, and all of my other relationships are viewed in that light. My oath to her has settled the question of "to whom do I belong?" I do not need to wonder where my home is.

My third oath is to Christ and his Church. As a member of the sacred order of priests, I have given myself to a single vocation. I am called to obey my bishop, to serve God's people, to preach the Word, and to administer the sacraments. This goes beyond mere employment. Though I may not work at a specific job for the rest of my life, the question of my calling has been answered. I'm simply a priest. I'm not looking for the next big thing.

My fourth oath is my oblation to the Monastery of Christ in the Desert. I intentionally connected myself to that community and am a secular brother. That means that I have promised to live my life, to the best of my ability, according to the Rule of St. Benedict.

My first three oaths govern my daily life. Who I am as a Christian, a husband, a father, and a pastor are wrapped up in these vows. I did not need to take on a fourth oath. However, my Benedictine vow has brought a texture to my life that I am deeply grateful for. The Benedictine way includes a rhythm of life; a deep valuing of prayer, silence, and work; and a serious call to hospitality. These, and other gifts, are important to me. But of all the gifts, the one I most wanted to share with you has to do with the vows themselves.

In the Rule, St. Benedict insists that his monks vow three things: obedience, stability, and conversion-of-life. These vows have been enormously helpful to me, and I'd like to tell you why. When I'm confronted with a decision, especially one of significance, I always go back to these vows. I have promised to be stable. This means that my default setting should be to keep doing what I'm doing. This comes up over and over in work, in relationships, in parenting, etc. I don't need to find the next cool thing, the next product, the next friend, or the next job. I am happy with where I am and whom I am with.

The vow to conversion-of-life pushes up against the vow of stability. It reminds me that God is not finished with me. My soul is not yet fully formed in holiness. He has set me on a course, but he can still give new direction. While committed to stability, I must always be open to what he may do next, or what he may call me to do. God has more renewal, more revival, and deeper repentance for me. He is always reforming me.

So, what happens when stability and conversion argue? How do I know if a choice is a temptation to instability, or an invitation to conversion, or both? That is where obedience comes in. Of course, I am already committed to obedience in my other vows, but this Benedictine rule pushes me from theoretical to actual obedience.

For me, obedience means I must seek both the advise and direction of those I am submitted to, as well as those I most trust. The first of these is, of course, Christ himself. So the Bible and the teachings of the Church guide and rule. Among humans, I am mutually submitted to my wife, Laura. She is the first person on my short list of obedience. Then there is my bishop, and whatever ministers he has placed above me in the church hierarchy. I am also blessed to have three dear brothers in Christ, three men whom I trust completely in all things. If I need direction, which I often do, I have these resources to guide me in the way of Jesus.

I suspect that most people live their lives according to vows, in one way or another. Some of these may be vows that are doing more harm than good. Vows made in childhood, such as to never trust another person, or to survive no matter what, or to become a big-deal, are destroying souls right now. Other vows are good, but are not being honored. Vows of marriage come to mind, as do vows of obedience, friendship, and parenthood. Some people feel lost in life, having no base. Perhaps returning to a vow, or taking on a new one, would be helpful. My sense is that many of us ask questions that no longer need to be asked, because we have already taken oaths and made promises in these areas (family, work, church, etc.). Others of us need to ask more important questions than we are asking.

The reason I'm writing all of this is to encourage you, the reader. I don't expect anyone to take on the four vows that I live with. Of course, I would recommend baptism and life in Christ to anyone, but the other three may not be for you. Fair enough. But I would ask you to consider what vows you are living under, and how those vows interact. Do you know what your boundaries are? Do you have a way to make important decisions? What steps might you need to take to enter more fully into your oaths? Who and what are you called to be faithful to? Who is already faithful to you? My hope is that you will ask yourselves these questions and be strengthened in the loyalties you already have.

Finally, I know that tragedy is always looming. The man who baptized me, along with one of the men who presented me for baptism, is dead. The bishop who confirmed me is dead. Some of the people I have baptized are dead. Some of the people I have helped join in marriage are now divorced. It is possible that one or both of my children will die before me. I am happily married to my wife, but that does not mean tragedy cannot strike. Our marriage will surely end in death. I am an ordained priest, but I don't know that I won't get fired, that my church won't collapse, or that my denomination won't disintegrate. I don't know that I will always be paid to do pastoral work. I am a Benedictine brother, but the monastery could change so that I would have to leave it.

What I mean to say is this: every person, every relationship, and every institution is subject to the forces of chaos and death. The people I am bonded to might go away, or I may be forced to go away from them. My settled answers could be denied, and I could be tossed back into unsettling questions. That is why it is so important that my vows are made first and foremost to God himself. My baptismal vows, my marriage vows, my ordination vows, and my oblation vows are all made to Jesus first. He is my guarantor, he is my partner, and he is the faithful party. Even if (and when) all else fails me, he never will. And so I live out my vows (very imperfectly) in trust. Not trust in myself, nor in my relationships, nor in my institutions, but in my Lord and Savior.

Fact: Thomas McKenzie once blew up a gas station. He has vowed not to do it again.

AN OLD HUSBAND OFFERS THANKS
by Jonathan Rogers

H er legs are as long as they ever were.
With each passing year she grows cleverer.
Things change, yet still she is forever her.
And her legs are as long as they ever were.

Fact: Jonathan Rogers once befriended a young alligator and civilized it. After it graduated college, it disowned its adoptive father and returned to the wild, thus proving the old adage: Never invest in the betterment of a surly reptile.

FOR JAMIE
by Andrew Peterson

Y ou are beautiful in ways
You cannot see. Beautiful
In light and motion and grace,
In patience, in the little
Smile that is your first instinct
When you're anxious or happy,
Or shy--even sad. In fact,
Your loveliest smile may be
The one you show me then:
When all that is left is you,
When at last your strength is spent,
When the plant has lost its bloom,
When you can no longer pretend
That your fear has no power;
Then, my love, you reach the end
And I can see your finest flower.

Fact: Pete Peterson once buried a chest full of treasure in the woods near Live Oak, Florida. He has lost the map, but the chest is still there . . . waiting.

BEACONSFIELD
by G. K. Chesterton

You probably have no idea that you are holding in your hands a piece of history. What you're about to read is an essay by G. K. Chesterton which has never before been published. That means you, dear and discerning reader of the Molehill, are among a very small number of people to have read the following words from the brain of one of the world's wittiest, most prolific, and most gargantuan people. I happened upon the original typescript—possibly typed either by Gilbert or his dear wife—and was able to acquire it earlier this year before the other bidders realized what a treasure it was. The pages, which include Gilbert's personal edits and his signature at the end, were folded in half twice, then presumably shoved into an envelope and sent by courier through the streets of London to the magazine for which it was written—though apparently the magazine never used the essay. After more than a hundred years, those four pages traveled across the Atlantic ocean and ended up in my possession, so it is with great satisfaction that we present "Beaconsfield," an essay by G. K. Chesterton, about his hometown.

—Andrew Peterson

The heart of Beaconsfield is the old cross-roads, which make visible and vivid its old character and function in the countryside. In this connection there are two main facts to be fixed; that it was a famous coaching stage, the first important stage on the road to Oxford; and that it was a true market-place used for markets and fairs. Both these facts involved truths of a more general sort that are not always understood under the limitations of more modern times.

First, it has to be remembered that railways have made the English roads much less lively and more lonely. A man in the Middle Ages going from London to Oxford, as multitudes of men must have gone to the popular medieval university, would have found the road much more full of life and traffic than he finds it today. It is notable that in all the medieval descriptions of ways and wayfarers, as in the Canterbury Tales, in all the medieval pictures of ways and wayfarers, as in the pictures of the Magi or of pilgrims to a shrine, the one touch that is always absent is precisely that touch of Byronic solitude which modern people vaguely associate with a barbarous age. The men of that age seem always to have thought of a road as a thing with people moving on it. This character lingered with various modifications, down to the last years of the eighteenth century, when the most familiar historical associations of Beaconsfield were formed. Beaconsfield in the time of Burke, as in the time of Waller, was almost certainly a busy place. It was indeed a small place; but it was a small place on a great thoroughfare, and a popular one. It is said that at one time as many as twenty coaches went by in the day. That goes considerably beyond our very reasonable train service; and in comparison the new omnibuses are few and fugitive and timid like the first butterfly.

The other fact to remember is what was really meant by a market and therefore by a market-town. Here again it is necessary to get rid of the provincial prejudice which some have called progress and see the post in its real scale. Perspective is an illusion; an illusion in history as it is in optics. It is no more true that a medieval market was musty or trivial or obscure because it is in the historic distance than it is true that a tree is really the size of a dandelion because it is on the horizon. It is no more a fact that a custom must be a failure because it is far in the past than that a man must really be a pygmy because he is a long way up the road. And there is no better example than the highly practical medieval tradition of the market in the fair. The common sense of Cobbett pointed out a hundred years ago that the method of markets and fairs is really far more practical and business-like than the method of shops and stores. Men come in from the farms and country hamlets, carrying things they have made themselves under the healthy conditions of country work. And in the market the practical man who makes the thing sells it to the practical man who uses it. There cannot be anything more businesslike than that; and compared with it all that we call business is an aimless bustle about imaginary things, adding up abstract figures and exchanging ceremonial documents. The man who sells does not have to rent a whole house over him while he sells a box of matches or a pair of bootlaces and the matches. No fact of economics could be simpler or less sentimental than that. But the common sense of Cobbett was too colossal to be seen. The dingy industrial magnates and individualist sages who disregarded him were really like pigmies playing on a giant so large as to look like a landscape. Today those enormous simplicities are beginning to dawn on men once more; and though nobody supposes that all historic processes should be reversed or all historic conditions restored, everybody is learning enough to look with a new sort of respect at such an ancient forum of four roads in the heart of an English parish, and to hope to see another fair in Beaconsfield.

Considering these to facts as the constant factors, the highway and the market, we shall find the historic features of such an old town falling into their place. It is true that the medieval past of such a place is now mostly attested indirectly, by things that are like the echoes of echoes or the shadow of a shade. The lost greatness of the monastic foundation of Turnham lies indeed like a sort of shadow over all this land; and some of the legends and relics of the Old Rectory attest to the last memories of that tradition as it died in the Tudor time. Perhaps the most vivid relic of it is really in the mere name of Candlemas Lane; and anybody who has read anything of the old village customs of Candlemas Day, when processions passed down the lane, may find his fancy visited as by the ghost of a girl with lighted candles in her hair. No one who has not seen such ghosts has any right to judge even of the names, let alone the things, of an old English town.

But though it may be no more than a coincidence, it has a significance almost amounting to mockery, that two of the most medieval of tavern signs hang out like banners above a tilting-yard, above the open space of the cross-roads. Indeed, one might almost fancy that the two inn-signs were brandished like banners in defiance of each other; for they represent emblems familiar to medieval civilization as mortal foes. One is the Saracen's head, the bogey of the old ballads and the Aunt Sally of the old tilting yard. The other is the White Heart that was the favourite badge of poor Richard the Second, and ultimately the shining symbol of the purity of the Blessed Virgin. These remote things should be noted because they are neglected; for the ordinary guide-book begins its real interest in Beaconsfield with the seventeenth century, where the more obvious play of local characters and scenes is apparent. The Cavaliers and Roundheads are all over this countryside, and all over the recognized books and articles about it. But the seventeenth century, whatever our sympathies concerning it, is hardly at present the model of social reconstruction; and I hope I may be pardoned if in my hopes for the remaking of England, I have looked back past the conventicle as well as the castle, to the market and the open road.

—G. K. Chesterton

Beaconsfield – an Introduction)
by G. K. Chesterton

The heart of Beaconsfield is the old-cross roads, which make visible and vivid its old character and function in the countryside. In this connection there are two main facts to be fixed: that it was a famous coaching stage , the first important coaching stage on the road to Oxford; and that it was a true market-place used for markets and fairs. Both these facts involved truths of a more general sort that are not always understood under the limitations of more modern times. First, it has to be remembered that railways have made the English roads much less lively and more lonely. A man in the Middle Ages going from London to Oxford, as multitudes of men must have gone to the popular medieval university, would have found the road much more full of life and traffic than he finds it today. It is notable that in all the medieval descriptions of ways and wayfarers, as in the Canterbury Tales, in all the medieval pictures of ways and wayfarers, as in the pictures of the Magi or of pilgrims to a shrine, the one touch that is always absent is precisely that touch of Byronic solitude which modern people vaguely associate with a barbarous age. The men of that age seem always to have thought of a road as a thing with people moving on it. This character lingered, with various modifications, down to the last years of the eighteenth century, when the most familiar historical associations of Beaconsfield were formed. Beaconsfield in the time of Burke, as in the time of Waller, was almost certainly a busy place. It was indeed a small place; but it was a small place on a great thoroughfare, & a popular one. It is said that at one time as many as twenty coaches went by in the day. That goes considerably beyond our very reasonable train-

service; and in comparison the new omnibuses are few and fugitive
and timid like the first butterfly.   The other fact to remember
is what was really meant by a market and therefore by a market-town.
Here again it is necessary to get rid of the provincial prejudice
which some have called progress; and see the past in its real
scale.   Perspective is an illusion; xxxx an illusion in history
as it is in optics.   It is no more true that a medieval market
was musty or trivial or obscure because it is in the historic
distance than it is true that a tree is really the size of a
dandelion because it is on the xxx horizon.   It is no more
a fact that a custom must be a failure because it is far in the
past than that a man must really be a pygmy because he is a long way
up the road.   . And there is no better example than the highly
practical medieval tradition of the market in the fair.   The
common sense of Cobbett pointed out a hundred years ago that the met
method of markets and fairs is really far more practial and
business like than the method of shops and stores.   Men come in
from the farms xxx and country hamlets,carrying things they have
made themselves under the healthy conditions of country work.
And inthe market the practical man who makes the thing sells it
to the practical man who uses it.   There cannot be anything
more businesslike than that; and compared with it all that we
call business is an aimless bustle about imaginary things, adding
up abstract figures and exchanging xxxxxxxxxxxx ceremonial documents .   The
man who xxxx sells does not have to rent a whole house over him ,
while he sells a box of matches or a pair of bootlaces.   The
man who buys does not have to pay extra for the house as well as
for the bootlaces and the matches.   No fact of economics could
be simpler or less sentimental than that.   But the commonsense

of Cobbett was too colossal to be seen.   The dingy industrial
magnates and individualist sages who disregarded him were really
like pigmies playing on a giant so large as to look like a landscape.
Today those enormous simplicities are beginning to dawn on men once
more; and though nobody supposes that all historic processes should
be reversed or all historic conditions restored,everybody is
learning enough to look with a new sort of respect at such an
ancient forum of four roads in the heart of an English parish,
and to hope to see another fair in Beaconsfield.

     Considering these two facts as the constant constant
                      way
factors, the high road and the market,we shall find the historic
features of such an old town falling into their place.   It is
true that the medieval past of such a place is now mostly attested
indirectly, by things that are like the echoes of echoes or the
shadow of a shade.   The greatness lost greatness   of the
monastic foundation of Burnham lies indeed like a sort of shadow
over all this land; and some of the legends and relics of the
Old Rectory attest to the last memories of that tradition as it
died in the Tudor time.   Perhaps the most vivid relic of it
                                            and
is really in the mere name of Candlemas Lane; as anybody who has
read anything of the old   village customs of Candlemas
Day, when processions passed down the lane, may find his fancy
visited as by the ghost of a girl with lighted candles in her hair
No one who has not seen such ghosts has any right to judge even of
the names names,let alone the things, of an old English town.
But though it may be no more than a coincidence, , it has a signif
significance almost amounting to mockery , that two of the most
medieval of tavern signs hang out like banners above a tilting-yard,

above the open space of the cross roads .   Indeed, one might almost
~~xixst fxny~~ fancy that the two inn-signs   were brandished like

banners in defiance of each other; for they represent emblems

familiar to medieval civilisation as mortal foes .   One is the
and
Saracen's Head, the Bogey of the old ballads ~~an~~ the   Aunt Sally

of the old tilting yard .   The other is the White Hart that was

the favourite badge of poor Richard the Second, and ultimately

the shining symbol of the purity of the Blessed Virgin.   These

remote things should be noted because they are neglected; for the

ordinary guide-book begins its real interest in Beaconsfield

with the seventeenth century, where the more obvious play of

local characters and scenes is apparent.   The Cavaliers and
and
Roundheadds are all over this countryside , ~~an~~ all over   the

recognised books and articles about it.   But the seventeenth

centruy, whatever our sympathies concerning it, is hardly at
the model
present ~~thxmad~~ of social reconstruction; and I hope I may be

pardoned if in my hopes for the remaking of England , I have

looked back past the conventicle as well as the castle, to the

market and the open road.

G. K. Chesterton

THE GARDEN HOUSE
by Andrew Peterson

I want to shape the land on which I live,
but only if by shaping
I love those who come after, and those
who came before.

Our house, they tell me, was built
where the old garden sat.
That has always struck me
as a beautiful fact,
and it's nice to imagine
some mystical blessing
rising from the fertile soil
beneath the foundation,
coursing through our veins
and to the tips of our fingers
and toes while we sleep,
a natal benediction spoken

over us by the light
of a heavy-lidded moon.

I step out of the house
come morning, my body a vessel
of seed and color and sunlight,
broken open by the hands
of harvest, to nourish
the ground around me,
to feed and be fed, then to lie down
again in the raised bed, spent,
content, tired, hungry, happy.

I want to shape the land on which I live,
But only if by shaping
I love those who come after, and those
Who came before.

MAKING PEACH COBBLER
by Jen Rose Yokel

Soft velvet peel,
fragrant as summer,
slides into the bowl
in imperfect strips,
and the soft, yellow flesh
leaks nectar down my forearm.

I am making peach cobbler
much like my grandma once did.

I dig the knife in
and wrangle one
jagged, slippery slice
into the bowl,
then rip another
from the pit.

A friend asked me later
how I found peaches
in New England.

Who knows how they traveled so far,
foreigners in a Walmart bin.

Fruit of the South,
or a nursery nearby,
or greenhouse?
Who knows?

All I know is
I am making peach cobbler.
The blade nicked me once,
and I squeezed a wet napkin
around the cut.

The peach slices
are boiling in sugar,
however they got here,
however I got here,

wandering far
to fill a home
with a fragrant offering.

ROYAL PRIESTHOOD
by Chris Yokel

Everyday he walked
morning-misty streets to the factory,
punched his card with calloused fingers,
and took his place at the conveyor belt.
It was a sanctuary of industry,
Sunlight slanting down through
high windows,
dust-motes glimmering gold,
falling
like manna on the lowly men and women,
the mechanical rhythm of clack and clatter
rising to meet it in murmured prayer,
as his fingers blessed each box in passing.
And when the day chimed out,
his card punched,
factory departed,
he walked the streets back home,
his face shining like Moses.

Fact: Chris Yokel has a secret code word. If you say it to him three times quickly, he will do a somersault and shout "Bring me the monkey!" We can't tell you what it is, but it rhymes with "snickerdoodle."

MISS PORK CUISINE
by Russ Ramsey

From my chair on the sidewalk in front of the bank,
I watch as this year's Miss Pork Cuisine glides past
waving from her perch atop the trunk of the local dentist's convertible.
The Shriners figure eight in choreographed glory behind her,
their miniature motorcycles like the train of her robe filling the parade
    route.

She is to this town what the car she sits upon is to the dentist,
an achievement in beauty and refinement,
a symbol of youth,
this year's model,
one of the noticed few.

I wave back telling her to enjoy the ride.
The parade seems to be moving slowly,
but it will be over before she knows it.
There will be another next year
but it will not belong to her.

Fact: In high school, Russ Ramsey was the reigning Pound Cake King for three years running—O, how the tasty have fallen.

and other recipes by Lewis Graham
(with illustrations by Jennifer Trafton)

It's getting to be about chili weather. Or it is while I'm writing this, so if it's July when you finally get around to reading your copy of the Molehill then skip over this one until October. Also, stop procrastinating. What if Jesus had come and you didn't get to make any chili?

Store Run:
   1 large yellow onion, chopped
   4-5 cloves garlic, minced
   1 jalapeño pepper, finely chopped
   1 Serrano pepper, finely chopped
   1 poblano pepper, finely chopped
   *if chili is for John Barber, come see me for some ghost chilies.
   16 oz ribeye steak, cubed

1 lb chuck flap, cubed
1 lb brisket, cubed
2 16oz cans red beans, drained
2 16oz cans kidney beans, drained
2 16oz cans some other kind of beans, drained. It's late, and its been
    a long week.
1 bottle plain yellow mustard
2 tablespoons ground cumin
2 tablespoons Mexican oregano
2 tablespoons kosher salt
2 tablespoons black pepper
2 tablespoons coriander
2 tablespoons red pepper flakes
2 tablespoons smoked paprika
1 large can of whole, peeled tomatoes
Six pack Yazoo, Dos Perros, or a full body Pinot Noir or Cabernet

Take your cubed meats and season them first with salt and pepper. Now, you could grind them. If you are so inclined, grind them once, mix them all together, then grind them again. If you choose not to grind them, cut them up however you want to—it's your world. Fire up a heavy bottom skillet and put a couple glugs of good olive oil in the bottom. Just as it starts to smoke add your beef. Yes, you could use ground turkey instead.

Leave it alone now. Let it brown. Once the meat is nice and browned remove it and drain off the excess grease. Reserve a little meat grease and put it back in the pan.

Add your onions, peppers, and garlic and sweat them. Sweat is a very technical kitchen term that means cook them some, but not too much. Now, add your beef that you're standing there eating to the pepper mix. Throw in the seasonings and mix it all together.

I like to use a crockpot, but you could go stovetop if you insist on hanging around and stirring chili all day.

Put the beans in the pot along with the meat. Take your can of tomatoes and pour the juice in. Take each tomato and squeeze it.

Reader's tip: do this gently—as they are full of juice. If you squeeze them too hard, juice goes everywhere and your wife will be hollering for days. Or, squeeze the tomato in the direction of said wife, and try not to laugh whilst being flogged.

Let everything go for as many hours as you can stand, at least three. Taste often and season as you wish. At some point, throw a shot of yellow mustard in there. If you can't taste the difference add some more. If you can taste the mustard you added too much and you'll have to wait for the Molehill vol. 4 to find out to un-mustard your chili.

I always have a radio in the kitchen. However, chili day is usually a Sunday and our house is kinda quiet of an evening. So hang out with your people and watch a movie. I find few things more comforting than the smell of chili cooking, a good movie going, and the dryer running in the background.

Pro tip: Finish your chili off with fritos, sour cream (which I always forget), and some sharp cheddar cheese.

LET'S MAKE CRAB CAKES

S*hopping list:*
3 lbs jumbo-lump crab, picked*
2 poblano peppers, finely diced
1 yellow onion, finely diced
2 red bell peppers, finely diced
1 bunch cilantro, stems removed, chopped
3 cloves garlic, minced
2 cups mayo **
2 cups panko
2 tablespoons cajun seasoning
1 whole lemon
Amos Lee—Mission Bell
Jason Isbell—Southeastern
Hozier—Hozier

Chilled, oaky Chardonnay, or a cold, cold IPA

*Yes, claw is cheaper, but it isn't wise to shave corners on attorneys, tattoos, or crabmeat.

**Recipes are suggestions, except when it comes to mayonnaise. Miracle Whip isn't mayonnaise.

Order of Things to Come:

1. Take your finely diced vegetables and give them a good sauté in butter or olive oil. When the onions start to soften, add the garlic and season with kosher salt and black pepper.

2. When the peppers are pliable and onions translucent, spread the mixture out on a cookie sheet and place in refrigerator to cool.

3. In the interim, pick through the crabmeat and discard any bits of remaining shell. In a large bowl, mix the crabmeat, cajun seasoning, cilantro, and panko.

4. Add your cooled vegetables to the bowl and mix well.

5. Take a break. Go outside for a minute, clean up your station, get squared away.

6. You can make these as large or as small as you choose. I usually go about two ounces each. Kinda ball 'em up, then flatten them just so. Make a circle with your thumb and pointer finger. Show it to someone, being careful to keep it below the waist. If they look at it, you get a free punch on their arm. However, if they break the circle, they get two licks on yours.

7. Back to the crab cakes. Take your finger circle and round out the cakes. You want to end up with a short, spool-shaped cake.

8. Now then, you have to cook them. Fire up the fry daddy, toss them in some panko, and fry them to a golden brown. Sadly, some people have sworn off the fried foods. So here's the quantity over quality method. In a non-stick pan, heat up some olive oil. Sear off both sides of the crab cake then put them on a tray in a 350° oven for about 12 minutes.

9. Serve them with a spicy remoulade, garlic aioli, tartar sauce, or get you some mango puree and mix it 1:1 with sambal (chili paste).

10. I mentioned a lemon in the recipe and just now remembered. Cut it in half and squeeze the juice into the crab mix.

Extra Credit:

Peel a sweet potato. With the same peeler, shave down the potato. Get a pot of water on and heat it to barely a boil. Throw your shaved potato into the hot water, then turn the heat off. Let them blanch for three to four minutes. Drain the water and pat the potato pieces dry. With your frier still hot, fry off the shavings a small batch at a time. When they are crispy, take them from the oil and toss them in a bowl with salt and pepper. Use them as a garnish.

CARAMELIZED CORN PUDDING

Maybe you have a potluck coming up and you want to be the belle of the ball. Or maybe it's a fancy dinner at home and you're going to get out the good china. Or even in the event the kids want pizza—well, one wants pizza, the other wants a cheeseburger—break out this crowd pleaser and drop some southern love on 'em.

You'll need :
   ¾ cup unsalted butter
   2 yellow onions
   2 poblano peppers
   1-2 jalapeno peppers
   5 lbs sweet corn (about 15-20 ears)
   1 cup Andrew Peterson flour (that's A.P.)
   1 ½ qt heavy cream *
   5 egg whites
   2 tablespoons salt
   2 tablespoons black pepper
   2 tablespoons smoked paprika

2 tablespoons minced garlic

2 tablespoons positive attitude

1 tablespoons dried thyme

1 tablespoons dried oregano

¼ cup sugar

2 cups panko

1 lb white cheddar

½ cup parmesean

*Don't buy the cheap stuff. Buy the high-fat, foreign-language, gotta-break-into-the-kid's-college-fund stuff.

Here's how:

Fix a glass of lemonade.

Put on some good rock and roll—The Black Keys, Foo Fighters, Led Zeppelin, The White Stripes, or whatever you like, as long as it's loud and you can dig it. If you don't like rock and roll, go buy the cheap heavy cream and hang out with your cats instead.

First, melt the butter on the stove. Wait—first, raise your right hand. Go ahead. I'll wait. Okay, now promise never to use a microwave for any recipe I give you. Ever.

Now, back to the butter. Sauté the peppers and onion in the butter. Now, you could add some bacon or country ham at this point. I know, I know, it's not on the list. Hang the list—go with

inspiration. You will add the corn to this mixture, but may I make a suggestion first? Fire up the grill, throw some hickory chips on the coals, and smoke the corn first. No grill, no problem. Crank the oven up to 400° and roast the corn, in the husk. Then shuck it, clean it from the cob (SAVE THE COBS!), then add it to the pepper and onion mix.

Once your peppers and such are doing their thing, add the flour. The mix is going to thicken, and you've just made roux. Add in the second-mortgage heavy cream, sugar, and seasonings. Remove from heat and let it cool.

Once the mix is room temperature, fold in the egg whites, panko, and cheeses. Place in an ovenproof dish at 350° degrees and bake covered for 45 minutes. Remove the cover and bake again until nice and golden brown.

Now, you can stop here. No one will think less of you. But let's say you want to go the extra mile . . .

Get a propane blowtorch. You could get a brûlée torch, and you could also buy an electric car, but this is America. So get the propane torch. Spread a layer of sugar across the top of your corn pudding. With a dry towel, hold the dish in one hand, and with your torch, begin melting the sugar. You'll have to turn the dish this way and that way to make it all work. Maybe you want to jump on Youtube and watch a couple of quick videos on how to brûlée first. As I said, it's totally okay to skip this step. It's tricky, and melted sugar can be very dangerous.

Right, the corn cobs. Bag them in a gallon zip lock and put them in the freezer. Later on, add them to any soup or stock.

Finish your lemonade and go get dressed. Your party is starting soon and you don't want to be too late. Practice humility—everyone is going to be asking how you learned to be the world's greatest chef.

Fact: Lewis Graham can get you a working refrigerator in 30 minutes flat. He can also help you throw it off your balcony.

Never, Sweeting, Could I Play Thee False
by Sir Richard Roland

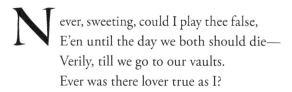

N ever, sweeting, could I play thee false,
E'en until the day we both should die—
Verily, till we go to our vaults.
Ever was there lover true as I?

Rocks may split, the mountains all remove,
Gone away the rivers, all run dry.
Only I will love still, still unmoved.
Never was there lover true as I.

Never, sweeting, could I make thee weep.
Away, away with each old love thou ruest.
Give me thy heart, and my heart thou canst keep.
I of every lover am the truest.

Verses sometimes lie; I never do.
Eye me, and the soul of truth thou viewest.
Yew bow never shot a shaft so true.
Of every lover, dear, I am the truest.

Until the end I plight my troth, forsooth.
Upon my hoary age, upon thy youth...
Prithee, hast thou ever known such truth?

—Sir Richard Roland (1587)*

* While doing research via microfilm in the Vanderbilt library, Jonathan Rogers came upon this hand-written poem in the margin of a sixteenth-century manuscript by a Sir Richard Roland, Second Earl of Astley. Apparently it has never been published, so this is a poem that few living eyes but yours, dear reader, have ever seen.

THE BLACK HORIZON (PART III)
Story and Illustrations by Jamin Still

BIRDSONG

Jacob sat at the top of the finished tower, in a room that looked out over the sea. He had brought his charts and instruments and papers up the night before and they now lay scattered across the floor. The plans for his boat were coming along. He had been spending his time at the docks lately with the traders and sailors now that the tower was done. He was learning what he could from them and felt confident about his progress.

Taking up his looking glass, Jacob peered through it to where three stars still hung in the early morning sky. Below them was a dark smudge on the horizon, almost like a cloud. He paused long enough to grab a piece of paper and make a note, bending close to see his markings in the dimness.

A piercing call cut through the morning air and a bird landed on the stone sill beside him. It looked at Jacob and said, "Why do you so often look to the West?"

Jacob opened his mouth and then closed it again. Then, "That's not your concern." He shooed the bird away and put his eye to the looking glass once more. The bird hopped down to a pile of papers and landed on an old folded piece of yellowed parchment

"Hey, get off there!" shouted Jacob. The bird didn't move. It simply turned its head and looked at him. Jacob hesitated and then swatted the bird away. He picked up the old parchment, tucked it carefully into his pocket, and then went back to his looking glass.

BROKEN GIFTS
by Sarah Clarkson

W hen I was a child, my mind was a gift.

Not the practical sort that parents exhort you not to waste, or a muscle to be stretched and kept. My mind was a gift of the kind that a grandmother brings when it's not even Christmas; undeserved, unexpected, a lavish glory of imagination that came to me like the first profusion of flowers in spring. I neither toiled nor spun for the splendor that grew in the plain soil of my little girl thought, but the inner realm of my mind and the restless imagination that roamed it like a summer wind was the secret friend and treasure of my youth.

My first years shimmer and burn in my memory, made almost surreal by the vibrancy of the imagination through which I beheld them. Tomboy and princess by turns, I spent a childhood catching tadpoles in the creek at the bottom of our street, climbing trees whose heights dismayed my mother, or twirling down the driveway in my current favorite costume. Mine was a world of tree forts and butterfly hunts and afternoons lost in my grandmother's sunbaked fields. But I was never alone and those simple pursuits always meant more than they seemed, for imagination was the comrade who capered and sparkled behind my eyes and kept an inner fairy tale at play in my mind.

The drama of that inner world spilled over the grass and gravel and sun of my ordinary backyard, making dryads of the trees, filling the sky with talking stars, making a heroine of sunburned little me on the commonest of days. I often returned from an afternoon at play with the wistful air of an orphan or the lofty brow of a princess in search of her lost throne. Sometimes the scenes in my mind spilled into words that I scrawled into half-baked poetry and wild stories about kindly unicorns. Sometimes they kindled a wonder that left me hushed and wakeful in my garret room, my thoughts long in the starlit nights.

Even then, though I could not have put it to words, I knew that my mind was a startling, powerful force. I felt it as a willful agent that seemed at times independent of my heart, a restless, curious presence that hungered for exploration. Daily, I was aware of my imagination as an ardent force straining against my skin, reaching out to grasp and examine the substances of life. Shaped by all it touched, formed by the beauty it explored, it also shaped in turn, forming my sight, honing my consciousness to behold the world with its own ceaseless curiosity.

As I grew older and age made a settled country of my mind, that restless power turned inward and the realm of my own soul became the roaming quest of my imagination. I discovered a hunger for God lodged at the core of my being. Imagination set to work and built a high, golden room around that desire and my soul often dwelt there as my thought reached out, not to the world I could see, but to the one that neither mind nor heart could yet imagine. Sometimes the silent concentration of that mental space seeped into the world as it had when I was a child, revealing not dryads or talking beasts, but a mighty Presence at play in the earth.

I remember a day in Texas when I was eleven years old. I ran through crackling, knee-high grass with grasshoppers whirring wildly away as I plunged forth in mad pursuit of a buckeye butterfly. With a mocking flit of wing, it outsoared me at last and I halted, breathless, hands on my hips, laughter on my tongue. My heartbeat slowed. The dome of the sky arced and shimmered above me; the heat was thick and golden, the air heavy with warmth and light. And abruptly I felt my mind gather its powers, summoning my attention to the vast summer beauty before me.

I obeyed, and my vision was honed, my senses heightened almost to fever pitch in wonder at the field that burned golden and wildflower red in the Texas heat and, like Moses' bush, was not consumed. My thought brimmed with the kind of wonder that slows time and for an instant, I was aware of God, awake to the love whose heartbeat is the pulse of the whole wide world. I felt a face behind that arcing blue, a face whose greatness stymied my waking sight, but not my wild imagination.

My mind, as you see, was my gift.

Until the day that it broke. And it was a gift no longer.

With the tardy wisdom of hindsight, I can glimpse the warning signs of a mind bound to stretch a little too far. The very potency of my imagination should have tipped me off, the way it shimmered and spun beyond my control, the way it sometimes careened into a dark region of thought that frightened me. Winston Churchill called depression "the black dog" but I would have named my spells the "black bird," for once in a long, rare while, foul, frightening wings dimmed the sky of my childish thought and the beauty of the world outside my eyes was obscured. I had nightmares. I panicked when I was away from home. Strange things sent me into days of vague fear. In those moments my mind felt like a piece of fragile fabric stretched almost beyond bearing, but the tension always ebbed before it tore and the beauty I found once more made me forget the fear.

I was seventeen when I woke one autumn morning with the images of a nightmare burned upon my thought. Neither in movie nor in imagination had I encountered the images of violence, the narrative of evil that my own brain produced. I saw the faces of the people I loved in shock. I saw images of death. And it seemed as if I had willed it, as if my own desire had caused the horror of the scenes in my nightmare. The ugliness of what I had seen appalled me, seemed almost to seep into reality. I took a deep breath on my pillow, gripped by the horror of what my imagination had set before me. It's just a dream, I told myself, just a dream. I plunged into my day with breathless energy, eager for sunlight and work to slough the awful pictures from my inner eye. I think I shook my head often, willing my thoughts to conjure something lovely, to banish the horror of that dream and with it, my sense of culpability.

But my thoughts wouldn't obey me. As the day grew, the web thickened. Eating or talking, walking or resting, the images of my nightmare pounded in upon my inner eye with a will all their own, smearing every scene of my ordinary day with their darkness. I could not stop or control my rampant imagination, I could not bid it to beauty, and as the day dimmed to nightfall and shadows pooled under the pine trees, fear pooled in my heart. I lay rigid in bed that night, fever heat on my skin as the images pummeled me and raged in my mind. I fought to stave off panic with prayer, for surely, I thought, sleep would heal me.

But sleep only slashed the last lines between my old self and the new, bewildered girl who woke to mental darkness and a mind that no longer seemed her own. As the fresh, clean sun slanted over my head, I looked at my hands as if they belonged to a stranger, so distant and detached did I feel from the self I had always been. I can't forget the date because in a strange concurrence of disaster, the rest of the world found itself shattered on that sunny September 11th as well. But before the phone rang or the TV screens screamed calamity, the world I knew was already lost because my own mind had betrayed me.

In the following weeks, I watched the grief of the wider world from what I felt was a vast distance. Day after day, second after second, the disturbing of images of my dreams beat upon my mind, seeming to associate themselves with the presence of anyone I loved, even as the images from the news filled my sight. Nighttime, dawn, midday, no hour or moment, however sacred, was safe. Prayer did not protect me. Church was no help. The furor of my unquiet imagination was a presence so powerful, I felt that I looked out at life through a dark fog that obscured the whole world and flattened every joy I knew. I don't think that words can suggest the terror that comes when you can no longer control your thoughts, when no amount of will power can keep evil images or mortal terrors from crowding your imagination. Night and day, the same imagination that had peopled the outdoors of my childhood with river folk and dryads now peopled my inner world with monsters. Once, my mind had shown me God, now it showed me relentless darkness.

I couldn't bring myself to confess these things so I drew deeply into silence, unwilling to leave the house. But I couldn't be alone. The long-beloved refuge of solitude had become a void in which my rogue thoughts screamed all the louder. I yearned for human company even as I shunned human touch for fear that my mind would contaminate those I loved. I kept my eyes down, my shoulders bowed, my hands tucked away. For even if my family was safe, how could they love me if I confessed what was ever before my eyes? I slept less and less. My whole body grew taut and weary with anguish. Slowly, my heart was suffused with the pungent air of guilt as I questioned whether those thoughts were my fault. With my own brain conjuring such darkness, could I really claim innocence?

It took two months before my lack of sleep so told on my health that I was forced, in wretched whispers, to admit my affliction to my mother. It took another two months before the darkness was given a name. "OCD" (Obsessive Compulsive Disorder) came the diagnosis in a chill white office on a day of deep, embittered winter. I scoffed at first. Weren't OCD people clean freaks and germaphobes who kept perfect homes and symmetrical walls? What relation did such trivial concerns have to the nightmarish terrors I suffered? Slowly, with precise articulation, the doctor explained that OCD came in many guises. Mine was "somewhat rare" in his learned opinion, but all OCD was characterized by the presence of "unwanted and intrusive thoughts" caused by a mind that had somehow gone awry, like a clock whose cogs had come loose. "The problem," he finished, with eyes of amused, clinical cool, "is that you're still sane. Your kind of mental illness doesn't disconnect you from reality. You get to know all the anxiety of a misfiring mind along with all the logic and reason of sanity trying to explain the inexplicable. No fun, eh?"

Indeed. The diagnosis was a relief, of course, because it banished my guilt. The dark world in my mind was not of my making, and that fact alone allowed me my first full night of sleep in months. But even as a modicum of calm nestled back into my heart, I faced the void of my future for the first time. For in "losing" the mind I had always known, I had also lost the world and self that came through it. Writer and dreamer, lover of God and the bright world he made, those familiar selves were nowhere to be found. I shunned the solitude and long walks I had always loved. I quit writing. The starlight brought me no joy. My mind was now a stranger whose presence I feared. And in those first days, I thought that it would never be restored.

The experts certainly didn't help me in this opinion. My parents, plunged into the bewildering world of mental illness, took me to a highly recommended Christian counselor. We sat in an office lined in theological tomes as a young, black-eyed man informed me that my trouble was that I was demon possessed. He pressed three books into my hands (and presented my mom with the bill). "These will help," he said. "They list every possible perversion your ancestors could have committed. All you have to do is figure out which sins they committed and renounce them. Then your sanity will return."

The next week we sat in the neatly ornamented office of a by-the-book psychiatrist, who believed in God, but didn't deal in demons. "Oh, I've seen so many creative girls like you," she cooed. "Don't worry honey, all you need is some good strong medicine and you'll begin to feel normal again. We have all sorts of depression drugs these days. We can get you in for treatment evaluation... hmmm... looks like we don't have an opening for another six months. I bet you can make it till then. Here, I have a book for you . . . "

As we drove home from Denver, I turned from the worry in my mother's face and peered at the long, icy plains in their surge toward the foothills. The wide, grey emptiness of winter pressed against my sight as I realized that no one would heal me. No one would mend my broken mind.

The work of remaking my life and restoring my mind lay in my own hands. And God's. The thought was automatic; faith was a habit I had learned early in my Christian family. But my soul recoiled at this, for the God I knew came dressed in the old joys of childhood, the beauty that I had lost. The faith of my parents no longer sufficed to answer for his current absence. A whole world had vanished with my broken imagination. In this new, stark landscape, I barely knew myself, let alone the God who had not kept my mind from breaking.

My eyes were cold and my teeth set as I stared down the horizon of my future. Adulthood lay just ahead, my eighteenth birthday, the age at which I had always assumed that the questions of childhood would be answered and I would step into a faith and a future of my own, independence in hand and the world at my feet. Instead, my coming of age in body and faith found me bewildered. It was almost as if I had to begin all over again. For though the troubles of my own life were enough to confound me, I faced them amidst the panicked grief of the post 9/11 world in which shattered hearts and war loomed large. My mind, I understood, wasn't the only broken gift. The world itself was a good thing turned bad. And what was I to make of it?

—⁂—

Funny, isn't it, how one broken thing reveals another?

As if one picked stitch in the cloth of normalcy is enough to unravel the surface of life as we are told it ought to be. My body followed my mind in crumbling, worn out by months of sleepless nights and acid fear. I laid dreams aside, put college on hold, and watched the future grow dim. I turned to church for comfort and found only pat answers and the slick, surface kind of kindness from pastors that I dared not test with my secrets. My friendships began to unravel as the eyes of my oldest comrades grew cool and careful at my attempt to explain what it meant to live and wrestle with a broken mind. The movie *A Beautiful Mind*, the story of the brilliant, schizophrenic scientist John Nash, had just released and I watched it with my oldest friend, hoping it would help me to explain. "But that's just weird," she said.

The world beyond my tempest in a one-woman teacup roiled and burned as well. Wars flared and deaths mounted. The end of the world was dolefully predicted. Heads were shaken at the battles of the coming years. At every turn, I met doubt and fear, and it seemed to slough away the smiles and ease, even the faith that I had taken for granted among those who loved God.

And I began to wonder if life was really, at core and bone, a cracked and battered old thing. Had childhood been merely delusion? Was all the beauty I thought I had known a sentimental mist cleared by the swift winds of pain? What was real? The glory I had known or the grief I now tasted? I snatched at the memories of childhood as if they were hands to save me, to pull me beyond the menacing currents of catastrophe into the calm of future hope. Surely, I cried in the dark nights, joy would one day trundle merrily up to my door and set her suitcase down in the empty house of my heart, returned at last.

But her journey seemed very slow. And the rooms of my heart filled slowly with the trappings of a new occupant; the languid, low-voiced ghost of disappointment. God, that vague, salvific concept, seemed as far from me as the high, hard stars I glimpsed in the long nights, his comfort as thin as the cold light they shed. Reason goaded me to belief in his being, but the new tenant in my heart suggested that his goodness, and all that hype about his being with us, had to do with beginning and endings, but had no place in the in-between. Life may once have been a gift, good in the long-forgotten beginning. Perhaps it would be good again. But life lived here, in the brutal world? It seemed nothing more than a pile of broken shards in my hands. This, I thought, is what it means to grow up and put away childish things. I grew very quiet. I was wont to wear black.

And then one, swift, chilled morning with a spring wind reddening my face, I visited an art museum to have, as Robert Louis Stevenson so starkly put it, my spirit "stabbed broad awake." This particular museum was in Poland, where I was visiting with my mother, exploring the country where she had lived and worked twenty-five years before. For days, we trekked the path of her memory down narrow streets and up the stairs into coffee shops with stained glass windows (picturing skeletons no less). To savor that world was to know my mother's story in a way I never had before, to taste a bit of the risk and prayer and love that shaped her missionary years behind the Iron Curtain. But our feet were tired one particular morning, our skin burned sore by the raw wind so that when we found ourselves on the stone steps of an art museum, we took their invitation up into the warm, gallery air.

I love art museums. I love to visit them especially in a country whose history I don't know well because the art of a people tells a story. It's not just the story of this war or that kingdom. Castles or knights, songs or families, the masterpieces a people create are the record of what they hope to remember, even when the rest of the world forgets. The story that day promised to be a lovely one. I walked into the main gallery, a room with a ceiling high as an old church, walls of palest gold, windows in the heights that let in a shimmer of morning light, and all I tasted was joy.

You could almost hear the laughter between those portraits—giant images of handsome, doughty men in military splendor, pictures of women with arch smiles and rich dresses, bold in their beauty and glancing toward the viewer. Landscapes stretched between them, verdant fields and orchards thick with ripened fruit and houses settled deeply into the earth. I remember the children best, the paintings of little ones in their gauzy dresses and billowy pinafores tucked in beside their mothers or in the high grass of a meadow or under the roses in a garden. I walked through the room, unable to rest for long at any one painting because each seemed to call to the other. The room was alive with the leap of painted glances, the echoes of timeless laughter.

I reached the end of the hall, and stepped into a small courtyard. Another door opened before me. Curious, I stepped through a much lower arch into the second, narrower gallery.

I stopped. To this moment of writing, I can taste the horror, heavy and sour on my tongue and soul that met me at sight of the first painting. Gaunt, bent bodies scattered broken over dirty snow, dull sky and hard walls hemming them in. I stared. Forgot to breathe. Began to shiver as if some door had let in a cold, cold wind. In a sort of mental shock, I lurched to the next painting. A picture in all blue tones of a boy with a whitened face and an absent air, black hair over eyes that did not even register fear from the guns pointed hard at his chest, or grief for the white body crumpled at his feet. I moved on. This gallery was long and low, the hall snaking ahead of me in shadow. The pictures loomed large on the walls in a silence that froze me still and trapped my feet until horror pushed me onward. The lines in each were stark, gashes of color sketching scenes of war and death in a mixture of strokes so swift it seemed the artist could not look long on his subject, wanting to escape the scene he crafted even as his own hand made it immortal. I felt the same, unable to look away, but longing for escape as I followed the gallery 'round. When the exit door yawned before me, I nearly ran for it.

In the little courtyard once again, crushed between the ghosts of what felt like two different worlds, I sat down. My mind could not reconcile those vastly divergent stories, for both told the tale of the same people. Two galleries. Two stories. One of a beauty so exultant it seemed indestructible. The other the tale of its breaking, a shattering so complete it seemed that the beauty never was and never could come again. The first, the tale of a golden age when the people inhabiting modern-day Poland had rivaled the kingdoms of Europe in splendor, the second, the tale of the ravaging loss that came with WWII.

What, I wondered, came after? When you have known such beauty, and felt such pain, what story do you tell when both are done? What third gallery was, even now, in the making, and what would its makers choose to tell with such opposing histories behind them?

What story would I choose to tell? Caught between those two vivid histories, I abruptly recognized myself. Those galleries embodied the recent history of my soul. Grace and grief. Innocence and despair. Beginning and seeming end. But neither was the whole of my story, neither the full narrative of the world itself. The world was good and the world was broken. But the breaking did not cancel the goodness as I had begun to think. Glory existed, vivid and living as those portraits in the museum hall. The joy I had known as a child was no phantom mist; it too told a story, made a gallery of reality as valid and true as the portraits of pain that came after. But both were incomplete. I stood now, perhaps as the Polish people had stood, as any country or human soul does after a season of war, with both childhood and battle behind me. Something new, something comprised both of beauty and pain lay beyond.

And in that moment, I knew that I could languish no more. A new set of pictures must be painted. I would craft and carve out a life after the beauty and breaking both. Something must be made afresh from the broken gifts.

But redemption was a word I couldn't quite comprehend at that point. Having heard it all my life, I associated it with what happened to people who had never heard of God, but I wasn't sure what it meant for a heart like mine, whose doubt was not in God's being but in his grace. When struggle and pain have tinged your every thought of God, how do you create new thoughts? How form a new vision of self? How weave hope from your few scant threads of remaining belief?

The empty hall of a third gallery loomed in my thought, a gallery whose essence was hope.

—⚬—

Three months later, I stood in church on a humid Sunday morning in Nashville. For the first time in my life, I was visiting an Anglican church. Having read great reams of Madeleine L'Engle, Tolkien, and C. S. Lewis in my months of darkness, I woke one day to the fact that they all were liturgical worshippers. I thought this must somehow inform the stories they told, the beauty they perceived, the hope in their work that was the essence of what I wished I could create within the third gallery of my heart. So I dragged my family down to the best known of the Anglican churches in Nashville, a tan-bricked, homey church with the affectionate name of "St. B's."

The beauty of it struck me first: the gem-toned windows scattering crimson and sapphire and emerald light over my face; the lit candles, the cross, square and center, almost a countenance facing me as I walked in. And the story—never in all my church-going years had I been so aware of enacting a narrative in the Scriptures read, the creeds affirmed, the prayers spoken in tandem with countless thousands around the world.

But my moment of epiphany came when I rose to receive the Eucharist before the altar. When I bowed under that cross, when my knees nudged the carpet and a priest kindly pressed the bread into my hands and whispered, "this is Christ's body, broken for you," the world, for one great remaking moment, stood still.

His body . . . broken.

Broken like the beautiful world he made, like the hearts of those made in his image. Crushed like my own hope, my own mind. Shattered like the countless thousands gripped by war. God's body—broken in and with the world that was meant to be his pure, wondrous gift. God's own body, at the cross, broken as a gift.

I held that bread and understood that the body of Christ was the last and final broken gift, the one that in a mystery, draws every broken thing into a love so mighty that death itself is turned backward within it. God with us in the broken world, broken himself, begins the remaking of the universe. I took the bread and drank the wine and in that moment grasped redemption perhaps more clearly than I ever had before. Hope, like a seed finally ripe, shot up in the soil of my heart.

I rose and shuffled off to the right, walking the aisle back to my seat, shy as always, but in that moment so brimful of my new understanding that I dared to keep my eyes up as I walked. My gaze was captured by the row of stained glass windows on my left hand side. A gallery, it seemed, of living light, reflected in the forms of diamond-eyed saints and ruby-hearted martyrs. Down the chapel they marched, a line of shimmering portraits amidst whose splendor I walked.

And then an older woman caught my eye on the right, with a glint in her glance as bright as the diamonds in the stained-glass saints. I glanced shyly at those in the pews. My gaze turned more thoroughly beyond myself than it had in many months as I beheld the odd assortment of humanity in the church that day; old and young, solemn or half-merry in their seats, every heart bearing both the grief and beauty of the human life that is a broken gift remade by a broken God. Every one of us had knelt, every one of us in need of the broken body of God. I felt a great camaraderie with the host around me. The sanctuary was hushed but it was charged with the energy of the hope given at the altar. Each person I passed, each saint in the stained-glass windows, was a living image of redemption.

And abruptly, I knew that I was standing within the third gallery I longed to create, right in that moment of sacrament and sight. I stood in a space of hope, a moment of eternity invading time, a place beyond the histories of sorrow, and my frail, beginning faith, and that space was crammed with the living images of redemption. The third gallery was here where the love of Christ invades the world, and the portraits were the living ones of the saints who are new creations of their God. I knew myself surrounded by living masterpieces, by our forebears in the windows, and my comrades in their pews. I knew that every one of us was a living picture of the Love who has come among us, our lives his portraits, painted in the vivid hues of redemption.

I got to my seat and lifted my eyes back to the altar. My imagination leapt to life and I was aware of my mind working within me once more as an agent of hope, a bearer of possibility. The walls of that place seemed almost to fall away, and a golden city rose beyond us, so that we in that room stood in a space of light and high ceilings and air that echoed with a music just beyond my hearing. Eternity was with us and the walls of time grew translucent. I couldn't quite see it. But with a mind held in the given life of God, with a broken imagination restored by the hope of Love, I could imagine it.

Unplug
by Chris Yokel

L ift your eyes to the skies,
and unshackle for a moment
from the modern machine.
Weary from wave on wave of
image and information,
let your eyes rest on infinite blue.

Watch the procession
of clouds across the sky,
or gaze on the sun gilding
a blade of grass.

Relearn the rhythm
nature taught you at birth.
Abandon the automaton
for earth's graceful dance.

Fact: Rather than being born, Sarah Clarkson, Lanier Ivester, and Jennifer Trafton were all brewed into existence by an elaborate china teapot.

ELEEZABETT AND JOHNNY LEE
by Walter Wangerin, Jr.

Sorrows are doorsteps;
Doorways are stories.
Who loiters on porches
Will get him no glories.

PROLOGUE

Before I tell you this story, I have to explain some of the things our great
grandfathers and our great, great grandmothers used to do when a relative
died. I will tell you about their "rituals."

It was in their kitchens that they prepared a body for burial, while the children sat among relatives in the parlor.

Sit quietly, children. Read the Good Book. Pray. Listen to the sounds in
the kitchen: the squeak of the hand pump, water flowing into the metal tub, the
cloth-washings of the corpse. Hush, and you will hear linen rustling as the women
dress your friend in clothes as sober as for Sunday church.

Listen to the men who are outside, sawing pine wood. Then hear the ham-
mering of nails to fasten the boards together. Do I need to tell you that they are

building a coffin of pine? Listen as one of the men is scrape-digging a grave with his spade.

Soon they will carry the coffin into the kitchen in which to put the body, then into the parlor to set both the box and the body on two sawhorses. They won't nail its cover shut until the morning when all the relatives and friends have come for the viewing. Still this evening you may look inside the coffin and see that your friend is very still and very pale. And blue are his lips.

Now many people come and sit beside you on straight-backed chairs and weep. They tell stories about your friend. Sometimes they laugh, because your friend used to be a funny lad. Mostly they are quiet, remembering. The parson comes in. He reads from the fifteenth chapter of First Corinthians, and, in a voice like a tolling bell, prays a number of prayers.

Finally, late that night, child, you are to be left alone. Two candlesticks burn at the head of the coffin, and two at the foot. The candle-flames cast weird shadows on the walls.

CHAPTER ONE

And so it was that young EleezaBett did sit vigil in the parlor by herself at midnight. The young lad's face had the cast of ivory. His hands were crossed on his breast. Shadows winked around his mouth, and shadows flickered on his brow.

Poor EleezaBett whispered, "Oh, Johnny Lee," for he had been her best beloved. "Oh, my handsome Johnny Lee."

Arms and neck, fingers and cheeks, the young man seemed to be molded of wax. Dead is dead, and what can be left then but memories and sadness?

"We laughed together when we were children," she whispered. "And we hid," she said, "in hideouts among the bushes. We walked and talked and held hands. We swapped dreams, you and I. Oh, Johnny, we had no secrets from each other, for we were the best of friends."

EleezaBett sighed. She was a girl too tender to bear the heavy weight of death.

"We thought our first kiss," she murmured, "was an accident. But it wasn't."

She sighed and smiled. "With our first and our second and all of our kisses we learned to love each other."

Chapter Two

Now, at the edge of town there lived a witch named Bella-Donna. Her hut had but one window. The door was built of oaken boards. It closed and opened with a braided leather latch.

She mixed potions, did Bella-Donna. She chanted spells. She brewed a cruel tea which caused those who drank it to confess their sins, which sins the witch saved in a little black box, for she might barter favors from sinners who feared that their sins might be known.

Enemies purchased her potions to punish their enemies. Husbands and wives dreamed bad dreams about their secret iniquities, so one would burn with shame while the other burned with anger. No man had the courage to condemn Mother Bella-Donna, and even the rowdy boys avoided her unhappy hut.

So icy cold was this Bella-witch that if someone touched her skin, his fingers would freeze and his joints lock up. She had hailstones, so the people said, for eyes, and her hair was a fright of icicles. When she coughed, sleet flew from her mouth. Fog blew forth from her nostrils like clouds. And hard as icebergs were her brains.

Poor Bella-Donna. She went about her business alone, always as lonely as pneumonia. When she came hobbling by down the road, parents snatched their children away.

The witch wished that someone might befriend her, but no one so much as came near, neither herself nor her little hut. If she could weep for misery—but she could not weep—her tears would tinkle like crystal ice at her feet.

There was, therefore, no reason why she should lock the latch of her door.

Nor could *she* give the first sign of friendliness, for her heart was a ball of cold, cold snow.

CHAPTER THREE

EleezaBett was bending over Johnny Lee's corpse. Oh, how she wanted to wail like a lost wolf cub. But for the sake of pale Johnny, and to honor his last night above the earth, she wanted to keep her vigil silent. So she bit her lip, and the lip began to bleed.

But she could not hold back her tears. Large, hot, wet drops fell onto Johnny Lee's eyelids. EleezaBett leaned down and kissed him, and her blood painted his pale mouth red.

The wet tears caused his eyes to flutter. Her warmth put a blush on his cheeks. And the kiss itself breathed life into his lungs.

Suddenly Johnny woke up!

He opened his eyes and looked straight into her. "My Bett?" he murmured. "My EleezaBett, is that you?"

Eleeza jumped back from the casket, and the candle-flames dipped in the breeze she made. How did . . . ? How could . . . ? But this was Johnny Lee's voice, and he was saying her name.

EleezaBett looked and saw that Johnny Lee was not moving, not a muscle, not a hair. Yet his eyes had followed hers, and his voice had murmured words.

"Johnny?" she cried at the top of her lungs. "Is that you?"

"Hush, Bett," he said. And he said, "I love you as ever I loved you before."

"Oh, Johnny," she cried, "Let's laugh and go dancing again!"

But Johnny Lee said, "There's no time for that. There's only time enough to tell you a terrible important."

"Don't tell me yet!" said EleezaBett. She wasn't ready for terrible things, and she feared that once he spoke it he would be gone again. Take all the time in the world," she pleaded, "before you do."

"Listen," he said, his body still stiff as a rolling pin.

"No! Not yet!" she said.

Johnny said, "I was murdered."

"Oh, Johnny—"

"It was the witch Bella-Donna that murdered me. With a sharp knife of ice she cut my heart out of my chest, and now she keeps it in a bowl of wine."

His voice was fading away. Her tears were drying on his eyes, and the blood was crusting on his lips.

Johnny whispered, "Go to the Bella-witch. Fetch me my heart. Put it in my chest again. . . ."

And that was all. His eyes closed, and his face was a mask of wax.

"No, no, no," Bett wailed.

She unbuttoned his shirt, and there it was: a deep cut, unstitched and yawning open.

Then all four candles blew out, and their wick-smoke curled into the air.

CHAPTER FOUR

What Johnny Lee Jones said—this is how it happened.

Bella Donna was sitting in her hut and thinking about the reason for her lonesomeness. "It's because of my heart," she said. "My heart is nothing more than a hard-packed lump of snow."

She thought some more. Cruel potions couldn't produce a blood-red, pumping heart. Sorceries were winter words, not summer breezes.

Finally the Bella-witch said to herself, "I have a plan. I know what I will do. I'll press an oil from the plant that gave me my name. Two drops, and a body falls to sleep."

She put the plant in a cider press and squeezed out exactly two drops. Next she took a glass jar down from a shelf and found a bottle of the best red wine, and poured it into the jar.

Early in the mists of the following morning the witch crept from her hut and hid in a ditch beside a winding road. She knew well what Johnny Lee's habits were.

Every day at sunrise he would walk his cows along this winding road, leading them out to a grassy pasture.

"Come, Bertha," he would say. "Come, Bossy."

But on this particular morning Johnny never got to the pasture.

Bella-Donna had legs like a donkey's. She jumped up from her ditch. She spat a drop in each of Johnny's eyes. With a stone she broke his ribs, and with her cold, cold fingers she plucked out his heart, then hobbled back to her hut.

That was her plan. She meant to put the lad's heart into her own frozen chest.

CHAPTER FIVE

While Bett was sitting vigil in the dark, there was no help for it, but that she fell asleep. Grief, you know, can make a young lass tired.

The next morning a loud noise woke her up.

"Johnny's cows!" she cried. "They came back all by themselves!"

She ran to the window and looked out.

But there *were* no cows. Only a donkey—and a tinker-man beating it.

"Git on with you, you filthy beast!" the tinker-man was shouting. His donkey was burdened with many bags. "If'n you don't git, I'm gonna be shut of you!"

Whack, whack! He hit his donkey with a dunder-stick.

The donkey brayed like a child in pain, but she did not move. Therefore the tinker-man looped a rope around her throat and began to pull—and the pulling tightened the rope, and the rope began to strangle the poor beast.

Bett raced through the kitchen and out the back door.

"Stop that!" she yelled.

But the angry man paid her no heed.

He yanked and yanked on the rope. The donkey bit the rope in half. So the tinder-man picked up a log.

"Die, you contrarian!" he shouted. "Die, you nit-bitten rogue, and I'll cut out your heart!"

He raised the log and gave the donkey such a clout that she fell down dead.

The tinker-man yelled, "I *told* you I would!"

He snaked a knife from his britches and cut through the dead donkey's ribs and ripped out her heart.

"Now I'm gonna cook your heart and eat it for supper!"

EleezaBett ran at the tinker-man. She slapped him around his head. She snatched his knife and aimed it at him. The lass was so wild with rage that the tinker-man ran away, leaving all his bags behind.

Then Bett went and picked up the donkey's heart. It was pumping with nothing to pump.

"Oh, sweet heart," she said. "What will I do with you?"

All at once Eleeza knew exactly what to do.

CHAPTER SIX

It was at noon of that very same day when Bett came to Bella-Donna's hut, carrying a small sack over her shoulder.

She heard strange sounds inside: *Chip-chip, chip-chip* and *Ouch!*

She went to the window. "Hello?" she called. "Does someone need help in there?"

Chip-chip—Ow-eee!

LeezaBett looked through the window.

There was the witch Bella-Donna, lying on her back on the floor. She was holding a mallet in one hand and a chisel in the other, and was banging away at her chest.

Chip! went the mallet, *Chip-chip* went the chisel, and the witch cried out, "Ow-eeee!"

Bett went to the door. She grabbed the leather latch and stepped inside.

"Poor, poor widow witch," she said. "Give me your mallet. Give me the chisel too, and lie still. I know what you want. I will do the work for you."

So EleezaBett put the edge of the chisel to witch-Bella's icy chest, then whacked and whacked and drove it in until she'd made a fair-sized hole.

"Now then," she said. "Where is the heart you want to put in?"

Bella-Donna aimed a crooked finger at a bowl on the shelf.

Bett smelled red wine. And in the wine she saw her Johnny Lee's heart. This she set aside. Then she held up a right strong heart so that Bella-Donna could see it—a heart that was twice as big as Johnny Lee's. Straightway, and like a surgeon of fame, EleezaBett planted that heart in the witch's chest.

CHAPTER SEVEN

In the waning hours of that same afternoon, all the townsfolk gathered on the road outside EleezaBett's house.

They had opened the bags of the tinker-man's tools and had covered a pine casket with a shining tin. On the tin they had inscribed the words, "Johnny Lee Jones. May he rest in peace."

These were the friends and the relatives that had sat with Bett in her parlor last night. Now six men lifted the casket onto their shoulders, three to a side. They staggered to find the balance. The parson took his place at the head of the casket, and then everyone began to walk to the grave that had been dug with a spade last night.

The parson read from his black book: "We brought nothing into this world," he read with a sonorous voice. "And it is certain we can carry nothing out. They that sow in tears shall reap in joy."

Directly behind the coffin walked Eleeza, and beside her walked a strange man who was dressed like a monk, and the monk's hood covered his face.

Soon the pallbearers were sweating, because the coffin seemed to grow heavier and heavier. Had Johnny ever been as heavy as this? No.

So the funeral procession moved sadly toward Johnny Lee's grave.

But just before they got there, they heard a loud *Bang-crunch!* The parson said, "Yipe!"

Two pallbeares had lost their grip. The coffin had hit the ground and cracked open, and a donkey's tail fell out.

A donkey's *tail?* Good gracious!

"Where is Johnny Lee?" the people yelled

"He's right here!"

Everyone craned their necks to see who had spoken. Why, it was the strange monk! The fellow threw back his hood, and there he was! It was Johnny Lee! As strong and as healthy as ever he was before!

EleezaBett laughed. She caught Johnny's hands. He whistled a tune, and they began to dance. For the lass knew, you see, how to stitch a good heart inside an empty chest.

"Parson," cried Johnny Lee. "How fast can you switch from a funeral to a wedding?"

Hee-haw! Hee-haw!

Way at the back of the long procession came the widow Bella-Donna, scuffing the road with donkey's hoofs, flapping great big ears, and singing "Hallelujah!" in the voice of a living donkey.

*Heeee-**haw**!*

> *Wash the windows!*
> *Sweep the porch!*
> *Heal your rib-bones!*
> *Praise the Lord!*

ANOTHER ODD COINCIDENCE
by Andrew Peterson

Another odd coincidence:
I read all week in the blue book—
The one Kenny gave me—
About longing. I followed
The reading plan: prayer
About thirsting to be thirsty,
Yearning to yearn,
Then Scripture.

"O God, you are my God.
　　　　Earnestly I seek you.
My soul thirsts for you,
　　　　My flesh faints for you
As in a dry and weary land
　　　　Where there is no water."

I read it every day this week.
This morning before church
I sat in my pajamas under
The wedding quilt and finished
The week's reading plan.

"Yes," I thought.
"These are good verses,
Good writings, good prayers.
I want to want you, Lord.
This is why you made me."

Then we drove to church.
I sat down in the pew
And Russ preached on
The lame man at the pool
Of Bethesda. He asked us:

"Beside what pool do you sit?"

Jesus asked the man,
"Do you want to be healed?"
And the man hemmed
And hawed, shuffled his
Useless feet. He wanted healing,
But not Jesus.
There at the pool
        He did not thirst
                For living water.

And so was my week of devotion
Perfectly punctuated. I sought
Spiritual formation. I sought
Wisdom. I sought inspiration.

And in this coincidence, not only
Do I realize the futility of seeking
Any good
    Without seeking
        Goodness himself,

I am smacked with the sense
That you want to show me
In this alignment of circumstance,
This cohesion of my reading
With the sermon I drove to hear,

That you are with me.

Emmanuel
    Is the bone-splitting Truth.
Emmanuel:
    God became flesh
        And dwelt among us.
Emmanuel:
    Every other doctrine
        Consummated in a word.
            In a name.

God is a God who wants
Me to remember,
And remembering, to believe,
That he knows my every cell,
Thought, and compulsion.
His life beats my heart,
    Binds my bones.

He is with me, with me, with me,
And I belong to him, belong
To him, belong to him.

What else is there?

What else could there be?

IT ALWAYS RAINS IN WINTER GARDEN
by Jen Rose Yokel

And a storm is never convenient,
so we run for the shelter of umbrellas
and storefronts, or wait in warm cars,
wipers clearing the intrusion away.

Summer storms come, fast and feral,
a whorl of wind, lightning, racing clouds,
and just as fast, they scatter.

But sometimes it's not all darkness.
The clouds like damp wool blankets
are wrung out, dripping over city streets.

Sometimes rain spills out with sunshine,
pouring down, mingling in liquid light.
It washes the dust from roof and road
and placates the thirsty earth

to raise gardens from our stone and progress,
to cleanse cities till they shine like new,
and to green a ravaged earth aching for
renewal.

The drops sparkle as they fill the air,
and still we wait it out—
while the world growing beneath our feet

raises its hands and shivers hallelujah.

THE COLOR OF SEPTEMBER
by Luci Shaw

The melon-colored harvest moon
polishes its way, arcing up through the branches
of maples, oaks, over the wooded summit
that forms the ragged hem of sky

The color of the month shows up in
a certain ripeness of heart and dryness
of touch. Bone-colored grasses blow
briefly. On my notebook's pale skin of
recycled paper I scribble what my fingers
already know—that shrinkage is tightening
the ruddy leaves like hands. Fertile summer's
already faded, yet here we are, still caught up
in remembrance, valuing for their persistence
one, another of the bright tissues whispering
to the ground, aged out of July and the flush of
their green juice, their stems too brittle to hold on.

The leaves drift down unknowing, destined
in just a few days for the burn pile,
a blaze that may, for an hour at least,
outshine the moon. Have you watched this
at your house? If not, tomorrow night,
go stand by the roadside where the leaves
accumulate, and wait for moonrise.

CANDLE OF PROMISE
by Chris Yokel

This candle of promise
is all my hope
in this winter of
dream's dying fall,
where dispirited trees droop
under icy weight,
breaking apart,
slipping into air,
sliding to the earth.

Here in these four walls
I can hear ice forming
all around,
the slow snake constriction
on branch and bush and water's flow.

I cup my hands around
this tiny flame of promise,

a warm globe
beating back the chill,
throbbing like a heart,
keeping life alive, if only
just alive,
but life enough to wait
in hope of spring's unfolding.

REQUIEM (*for Theo Rose*)
by Chris Yokel

H ere
in the graveyard
where the wet trees drip
onto stone half-shrouded in snow,

all the world 'round
bound in winter,
seeds frozen down in
the heart of earth.

There
across the stonewall,
the fields lay fallow,
brooded by mist,
taking their rest.

With the sun's slow turning
the harsh blanket of winter,

eventually becomes
the sustenance of life.

Now
in this chapel,
ceiling arches like dark ribs,
out of the depths I cry to thee,

out of this silent womb.

The colors of your light
stream through patterned glass.

Deliver.

Every tear from trees dripping on stone
takes life away from winter
and gives it to spring.

NIGHT STORM
by Andrew Peterson

I woke last night
At 1:48 a.m.,
To the sound
Of a terrible wind.

Jamie nudging
My leg with her foot,
The blinds bucking
Against the panes.

I leapt out of bed,
Slammed shut
The windows,
Knelt on a pile
Of clean laundry,

And watched
 The tulip poplar
 Bending low;
Listened
 To the rocking
 chairs bang
 against
 the porch;
Wondered
 When to act—
 When to climb
 The stairs
 And check
 The news
 For warnings;
Thought
 "On a night
 Like this,
 A spinning wind,
 A cloud-born,
 Howling dragon
 Could break
 This house
 And kill us all."
Questioned
 My judgment
 My courage
 My ability
 My discernment
 My faith, yes,
 And even God's
 Protection, both
 Now and after
 The Great Collapse

—and then the wind
Turned to rain.
The poplar stilled
and drank, drank.
Silent blue flashes
Lit the fields.
Thunder came
From far away
And murmured me
A goodnight song.

Fact: Matt Conner is a wanton fanatic of Operation Mindcrime. He has been programmed to recite its creeds from memory and can be made to sing them if properly provoked.

THE TIMELY ARRIVAL
OF BARNABAS BEAD
by A. S. Peterson (illustration by Jonny Jimison)

In the long and storied life of Colonel Barnabas Bead, there was no winter either so hateful or so magical as that which blew through the Cumberland Gap in the last days of 1864. It was aloof and amoral, as winters have always been, for while spring, summer, and autumn have their virtues and give their particular gifts of life, warmth, and beauty, winter abides no sentiment; she enters a room stiffly and coolly, quieting everyone to whispers, staring down her slim white nose as the world quivers before her. The season of Colonel Bead's salvation was a tyrant more uncaring even than all her sisters before. She hewed upon a direct line between political towers, taking no side at all, neither Union nor Confederate. In her march toward spring she laid men of all colors and creeds in their graves, and to look on her passage and see the sorrowful days of her procession, you'd not have thought anything good could come of her. But as December stretched its arms and yawned, there followed in the train of winter's gown a flicker of old magic that Barnabas Bead would not forget.

As Colonel Bead huddled by the dying embers of a fire in the shadow of Cumberland Mountain, he wondered not for the first time (nor the last) how he had ever strayed so far from the sea. His father, Howell Alan Bead (called Howlin' Bead by those who knew him) had been a sailing man and had spent his days before the mast fighting pirates in the first of the Barbary Wars. After the war, Howlin' had aimed to settle into a life of gentle labors and quiet days, but only a step from taking that well-trodden road, he had been diverted by the promise of a fair ship departing Savannah in search of parts wild and unmapped. The ship was a French privateersman by the name of *Esprit de la Mer*, and Howlin' Bead never spoke of his years aboard her without something very like a song in his voice, for he claimed that the ship had sailed upon the seas of other worlds entire, and plumbed the depths of lost oceans, and visited exotic lands that only the tales of Araby or ancient Homer rightly describe. In time, the *Esprit de la Mer* returned him to the shores of the known world and, having seen many mysteries to which no road leads, he put his foot at last upon the well-trodden path. He cleared an acre and built a house at the foot of Goshen Mountain, then he married a widow and founded a family which produced a long string of Beads that ended with the birth of Barnabas Alan.

In Barnabas' youth, his father had regaled him each night with tales of the high seas and all the fine adventures that lay behind him, and in his sleeping the young boy sailed a dreamland of his father's making. All his boyhood he waited patiently to be called away by the sea, but when, at the ripe age of twenty-three, he discovered that he had spent his youth in listening and heard no the call from the great deep, he left home to chase it unbidden. He bundled his few belongings and three strips of dried beef into a sack and stepped out onto the front porch of his father's house.

"Paw," he said.

"Why you got that sack?" said Howlin' Bead.

Barnabas shrugged. "Tell Maw I'll be back for supper." Thereupon, Barnabas Bead walked off the well-trodden path onto which his father had borne him. He took to the sea like Howlin' had, and while he worked as an able seaman on merchantmen between worlds Old and New, he kept one eye keen to every ship he met, wondering always if it would bear the name that carried the song of his father's tales: *Esprit de la Mer*. But the work of young seamen soon makes old salt of them; it wears dreams away as it does innocence and inhibition, and after years enough before the mast, then amidships, and then finally in staterooms of his own, Barnabas Bead grew lonesome for the well-trodden path and sailed for home.

When he returned from his long sojourn he stepped up onto the front porch of the Georgia farmhouse he had departed years before and dropped his sack. He saw his mother's form silhouetted in the window and called out, "I'm home, Maw. Is supper ready?"

His answer came in the form of a musket ball through the front window. *Crack* said the old muzzleloader, and *crack* said the window, and then "Damn!" said Barnabas Bead and down he went with an ounce and a half of lead ball in his shoulder. It is a terrible thing to be shot at all, and it is an even more terrible thing to be shot by an old woman whom you believe to be your mother—but is not.

The old woman waddled through the farmhouse door with a giant musket settled into the pocket of her shoulder. "You dead?" she croaked.

"I come to see my Maw and Paw."

The woman set the butt of the musket down on the porch floor. She reached into her apron and withdrew a powder horn and uncorked it and tapped a thimbleful of black powder into the muzzle of the gun.

"What are you doing?" cried Barnabas Bead. He lay sprawled on his back and held his right hand up to cover the thumb-sized hole in his left shoulder.

"I shoot any man comes on my porch without leave. Them as don't die, I shoot twice." She gnawed a patch of wadding off her apron and began to pack the barrel.

Disinclined to lie in wait of aid, Barnabas Bead leapt to his feet and ran.

What became of Maw and Paw Bead he could not discover, and he mourned the loss of his family so badly that he signed up for a new one: that of the Army of Tennessee. The army took him in without hesitation, sewed up his shoulder, and made him a colonel.

Soon afterward, the War Between the States caught up with Colonel Bead and dragged him wherever it went. On many a Sunday afternoon he led the boys and men of the Confederacy down back-country roads toward small towns and barren ridges that he was told (by General Felix Zollicoffer) would prove to be the very keys of victory against the North. But on those ridges and in those towns the war shook his boys and rent them, and though Colonel Barnabas Bead watched sharply for the gates of victory to open, he never saw the door crack an inch—though he did see many of his finest boys cracked open never-more to be shut.

By 1863 he had grown tired of chasing the keys of victory and he thought to get himself clear of the search by resigning his commission. He spent three days composing an elaborate letter of his intent and three days more working up the courage required to deliver it—during which time he often fell into heated arguments with himself.

"Barnabas, you've written the damned thing, and now you've got to march in there and give it to him!"

"I can't!" Barnabas wailed.

"You can!" Barnabas yelled back.

"He'll call me a coward!"

"I don't care what he calls us. We're tired and too old for this business."

"He won't care."

"Show him your teeth. They don't want colonels with bad teeth."

"That's true."

At that moment, Lieutenant Horton Adams, Bead's adjutant, happened to pass his colonel's tent. He overheard this argument and was determined to rise to the defense of the commanding officer he had served loyally for nearly two years. He flung open the flap of the tent and strode in with one hand placed threateningly on the hilt of his saber. When he discovered that the tent was empty—save only the man he'd entered to defend—Adams stopped short and held himself very still. In confusion, he cast about suspiciously with his eyes.

"What is it, Adams?" said Colonel Bead.

"I, uh—is everything all right, suh?"

"Of course it isn't. Why do you ask?"

"Forgive me, suh. I perceived that there was—ah, I thought I heard—"

"Look at my teeth, Adams." Bead leaned over (for he was considerably tall) and stretched his mouth wide open. Without hesitation Adams leaned in and inspected each tooth with the meticulous eye of an officer. When he had completed his inspection, he snapped his heels and grunted. "Well?" said Colonel Bead.

"Suh, yoo-uh teeth ah impeccable."

Knowing his teeth to be mostly missing or mostly rotten, Colonel Bead had not expected this answer. "Are you sure, Adams?"

"Yes, suh. They ah the teeth of a lion."

Colonel Bead picked up a hand mirror from his desk and inspected his teeth himself. "Adams, did you know that my father had a tooth made from the ankle-bone of a star?"

"Suh?"

"He was a sailor, Adams, and I was too, you know—but he sailed farther than any man I ever heard of. Beyond Good Hope, beyond the Galapagos, beyond India and Japan, even across the Sea of Tranquility—though he was never precise on where that was. He told me that he once came to blows with a man who wore a veil of fire and held a shard of lightning in his hand."

"Lightning, suh?"

"In his hand. Like a sword. Can you imagine that, Adams?"

"No, suh."

"They tussled, and when my father had nearly bested him (using nothing more than an old bucket and a yard of chain), a star fell from the sky and knocked out one of my father's teeth."

Adams sighed and his shoulders sagged and he smiled weakly. "You don't say, suh?"

"I do say, and so did my father, whom I never knew to lie. When the man with the veil of fire saw that the tooth was lost, he scolded the star and broke off a piece of its ankle, which he fashioned into a tooth and gave to my father."

"An incredible tale, suh."

"Here's a picture." Colonel Bead handed him battered old daguerreotype. It was a likeness of a well-aged man wearing an enormous smile, and set in the middle of the smile was a brightly polished metal tooth that shone like—well, even Adams had to admit that it had a star-like quality. Adams snapped his heels and grunted.

"Will that be all, suh?"

"Yes, very well, Adams. I have a letter to deliver. Will you excuse me? Dismissed." Bead looked softly at the daguerreotype and ran his finger across its silvery surface. *Esprit de la Mer.* He could almost hear the music of his father's tale. As he tilted the daguerreotype from side to side, the tooth twinkled at him. Then he slipped the picture into his pocket, took up his letter of resignation, and went in search of General Zollicoffer. The path between the tents of the Confederate camp was worn down to muddy ruts. Bead cursed the path and walked wide of it to keep his boots clean.

"Bead!" shouted General Felix Zollicoffer when Colonel Bead entered the command tent. "Bead, what are you doing here? Who's defending the ridge at Heathcliff's Bluff? Do you realize that Heathcliff's Bluff could be the key to victory against the North? Have you set picket lines? If the Union makes a show, it'll be hellfire and widows' weeping from here to the Virginia line! Zebulon tells me they've got three companies of artillery hid in these hills and his men have seen the ghosts of Hooker's cavalry galloping in the trees. Why, you must be a ghost yourself, Bead! That's it exactly, for I can think of no other reason why you should be here to haunt me other than that you are dead in the defense of Heathcliff's Bluff!"

"Sorry, sir."

"So you *are* dead then?" Had Felix Zollicoffer been a Catholic, he would have made the sign of the cross, but he was only a Congregationalist and didn't believe in the sign of the cross (or ghosts) so he took a drink of brandy instead.

"Well no, sir. I'm afraid not."

"Damn."

"Sir?"

"This had better be important, Bead."

"I'd like to resign my commission, sir."

General Felix Zollicoffer took another drink of brandy and then made the sign of the cross. "What did you say, Bead?"

"My commission, sir. I think I'd like to give it back. I've got an old shoulder wound, sir. I think I'd like to go back to the sea for a while. And I've got bad teeth, you know. Even Adams says so." Colonel Bead leaned over the desk and opened his mostly-toothless maw for General Zollicoffer to inspect.

In the twenty minutes that followed, Colonel Bead was called a coward, an ingrate, a damned coward, a blue-blooded sympathizer, a dirty abolitionist, a godless bastard, a Frenchman, a Tory, a Spaniard, a spaniel, a confounded boob, a congressman, a man of low moral character, a heathen, a papist, a Lutheran, and a good many other things that General Felix Zollicoffer could not pronounce correctly in his brandy-fueled rage. And though Colonel Bead was not permitted to resign his commission, he was immediately relieved of the keys of victory. General Zollicoffer reassigned him to a post from which he hoped Bead would never return and for which he hoped no useful commanding officer would ever be required. Within an hour of being shorn of his command, Colonel Bead, along with Lieutenant Adams (who stubbornly refused to be relieved of his own post), was marching east toward the Gap of the Cumberland.

"This is a good move for us, Adams."

"Yes, suh."

"A quiet spot in the mountains."

"Yes, suh."

"And when the war is sorted out, Adams, I shall take you to see the ocean."

"The ocean, suh?"

"Yes, Adams. The Atlantic."

"All things accounted, suh, when the wo-uh concludes, I intend to set fuh South Carolina."

"Of course, you will. I apologize, Adams. But if you ever go so far as Charleston, do go to the sea."

"Yes, suh."

"Did I ever tell you that my father was a seaman?"

Adams shoulders sagged and he sighed and he shook his head slowly from side to side. "No, suh."

"He sailed on a ship called the *Esprit de la Mer*. Isn't that a lovely name?" (Yes, suh.) "And he told me that the captain was a fiddle player. He'd wake in the night at times and hear her playing, the notes humming in muffled tones through the bulkheads."

"Did you say 'huh,' suh?"—by which he meant "her, sir?"

"I did, Adams. Indeed I did. He told me she had red hair and almost never spoke, though at night her fiddle spoke for her. He said the music of the fiddle drove the sails on windless seas and blew the *Esprit* to lands never seen by living men. What do you supposed he meant by that, Adams?"

"I don't know, suh."

"Neither do I. But I listen for the music all the same. I spent fifteen years at sea, Adams. I worked on seven fine ships, and had twelve able captains, and every night of those years I fell asleep listening for the music."

"Did you he-uh it, suh? The music?"

Colonel Bead frowned and looked down at his feet. "Are we still on the path, Adams? I lose sight of it sometimes."

"I believe so, suh."

Colonel Bead sighed and looked around him as if he had forgotten where he ought to be. Ahead of them the road weaved on through the hills, rising up toward higher crests in the distance. To the south, the land dropped away into a valley and the glimmer of water winked up out of the deepest reaches of it.

"This way, Adams. I suppose it's up this way."

They were four days on the road when they came to three shabby buildings that together accounted themselves the town of Harrowgate. The first building was a general store that was boarded up, disused, and guarded by a feral mule. Adams offered to shoot the creature, but Colonel Bead forbade him unless the mule should attack unprovoked. The second building was a wheelwright's carpentry that lay besieged by scores of lopsided, unfinished, and ill-engineered wagon wheels. The structure of the building itself seemed so inextricably supported by spokes, runners, and spare parts that Colonel Bead warned Adams not to touch any of them, fearing that the disturbance of a single wooden stave would result in an avalanche and put an end to one third of the town's infrastructure. The third building was an outhouse; Colonel Bead and Lieutenant Adams found it in working order.

The town of Harrowgate lay only a few miles south of the great Gap of the Cumberland, and Colonel Bead hoped to make a successful liaison with the townsfolk before continuing to his new post in the mountains.

"Is anyone there?" the colonel called out. He looked with great disappointment upon the derelict general store and its loyal guard, for he had hoped the close proximity of general goods would ease the difficulty of such a remote post. It seemed entirely likely to him that there lay within the building an abandoned sack of coffee beans waiting only to be reclaimed from ruin and put to good use each morning at breakfast. As he considered whether or not to brave the ferocity of the feral mule in order to mount an expedition of the place, a voice rose up in answer to his call.

"Which way you goin' to?"

Adams' eyes peeled back wide and white and he stared at the mule as if Balaam's own ass had come forth to prophesy against them. He raised his pistol and said, "Shall I an-suh the beast, suh?"

Colonel Bead took a step toward the animal and called out, "To the Gap." He spoke loudly, as though the mule might be deaf as well as vocal.

The mule bared its teeth and shook its head and bellowed a fearsome bray.

"I'd get no closer I was you." A stranger stepped from around the corner of the wheelwright's carpentry and shook his head at the mule. "He eat Cornelius three weeks ago. He likely take a bite out of you, you let him. To the Gap, eh?"

Adams lowered his pistol but kept his other hand on his saber. Though it seemed clear it was the man who had spoken and not the mule, he kept one eye on the beast and it dwelt under his suspicion.

"I'm sorry about your friend," said Colonel Bead, removing his hat out of courtesy.

"Him? He ain't no friend."

"I refer to Cornelius."

"Cornelius? Cornelius had it comin'. He'd crawl up on him and walk back and forth and pick and scrape at him and give him hell just for his own amusement. I knowed he'd get ate. Day it happened I heard him wailing. I come out to see was anything I could do, but he had him by the neck and shook him like a hound dog do a rattlesnake. When I come out again to go home he was swallered up clean and he been grinnin' about it ever since."

"Damn!" said Adams and took a sharp step away from the mule.

"Witness indeed that any man may come to an ignoble end," said Colonel Bead.

The wheelwright squinted and looked at Bead like he was an idiot, which he wasn't. "Cornelius was a calico tom."

Both Colonel Bead and Lieutenant Adams sighed, and Adams began to laugh nervously. Though neither of them approved of a cat-eating mule, it was a lesser evil than a man-eating mule-prophet, and so they chose to abide it without further interrogation.

The wheelwright slung a hatchet into the doorpost where it quivered and sang out like a tuning fork. He spat a rope of black tobacco juice into the dirt and wiped his chin, then he looked up into the mountain pass above the town and chuckled to himself. "You fellas do better to turn back than go up in that Gap."

"Do soldiers at the garrison come to town often? I'd hoped to find a trading post here."

"I don't see no one."

"Perhaps that will change."

"Uh huh. Old Lady Winter goin' to take up in that Gap soon, colonel. When she do she'll most likely keep whatever and whoever she find up there."

Colonel Bead considered himself well acquainted with "Old Lady Winter" and was concerned instead with how to get to his post in the Gap as quickly as possible. He frowned and looked around at the town. They had arrived on the road from the west. Another road departed east, and another crossed between the outhouse and the general store running southwest to northeast. Each of the three paths before Colonel Bead curled out of sight beneath the autumn trees and left him in doubt of which would take him up the mountain. The obvious choice was the northeast route, but many days spent marching blindly along country roads had taught him a valuable lesson: it is always best to ask. "The northeasterly road, here, where does that lead?"

"Where you want it to go?"

Colonel Bead smiled gently. "My aim is the Gap."

The wheelwright nodded his head and jerked his hatchet out of the doorpost. He cleaned the blade on his pant leg and sauntered into the middle of the road. "See there?" he said, raising the hatchet and swinging it in an arc that encompassed the countryside from southeast to southwest. Colonel Bead and Lieutenant Adams turned and looked. "Tennessee," said the wheelwright. "And look there." He pointed northeast and they looked there. "Virginia. And there." He pivoted on his heels and jabbed the hatchet northwest. "Kentucky."

"I see," said Colonel Bead.

The wheelwright chuckled and spat at the mule. "They's a crossroads, colonel. Places come from all over to sit down up yonder and meet and rub shoulders. This road. That road. You see 'em, huh? Me too. But they's other roads run all around. They run so thin, they go between all things, like spiderwebs strung up across a deer run and don't show but in the evenin' sun. They's roads all over, colonel. Some like this one—" the wheelwright stamped his foot "—well trod. Some others not so well. You fellas go up into that Gap, you take care. Roads up there get thin. The White Lady makes 'em even thinner. You sometime take off one way and get somewhere you ain't figured to end up."

Colonel Bead stared up into the mountain gap, and a sad, mournful shadow settled over his face. It was the look of a man for whom something precious had been lost but had also been forgotten and so is only mourned in brief moments when the wind brings him a familiar scent or the light reminds him of a barely remembered scene.

Adams looked from the wheelwright to the colonel in bewilderment. "Suh, if you could con-fuhm wheth-uh the road will go with-uh the colonel wills, we will be on ow-uh way."

"Take the northeast road, colonel. If you aim to keep to it, see you don't wander."

"Thank you," said Colonel Bead. "I fear I haven't asked your name, sir?"

The wheelwright grinned and spat. "Ask me again next time you come through Harrowgate." Then he retreated into his carpentry. The cat-eating mule bared its teeth and shuffled forward perilously. Colonel Bead and Lieutenant Adams took the northeast road into the Cumberland Gap.

Lieutenant Adams refused to pitch camp until an hour nigh midnight, and once they did stop, Adams looked down the road behind them at regular intervals to be sure the mule had not followed. They had climbed high enough into the pass that the warm air of early autumn had deserted them for more southerly climes. The wind that remained nipped and chilled, and Barnabas Bead felt in its touch the icy fingers of a dispassionate Lady teasing the hour of her advent. He kindled a fire to ward off her advances and leaned back on his pallet to sleep.

"We'll be there by noonday, I expect."

"I spect we will, suh."

"Do you suppose they'll be glad to see us, Adams?"

"I don't know, suh."

"I understand the garrison hasn't been reinforced in some time. The general told me the outfit is run by a young captain—his first command. I hope he doesn't take me as an insult to his dignity. You don't think he will, do you, Adams?"

"I spect not, suh."

"Do you see the north star, Adams?"

"Suh?"

"That one."

"Yes, suh."

"It never moves."

Adams narrowed his eyes and looked at the star suspiciously.

"At sea there aren't any roads to follow. Only stars. That's the thing about this Army business—I'm always looking down, looking to see I keep to the road. But at sea, you always have to look up. Isn't that something, Adams?"

"I suppose so, suh."

"Never mind your feet, Adams. Mind the stars. My father once told me he followed a star so closely that he sailed far enough to shake hands with Orion." Adams sighed and let his eyes slip closed. "I asked him how he got home again and he told me that it was no trouble at all, because from up there, the world too is a star, and one need only set a course to sail back to it. Do you believe it, Adams? Adams?"

Adams was fast asleep. Colonel Bead pulled his blanket around him and stared into the night sky until he slept.

The Appalachian Mountains spill down from New England in green billows. They wash over the continent in marbled swells of emerald and chartreuse, rising and falling, rippling through the bedrock with such patience and implacability that only an eye trained to the waver of eternal rhythms can perceive the cadence of their undulation; only the stillest ear can catch the thunder of their breaking and withdrawal.

In an age past, in the brief moment in which Cumberland Mountain rose up to the full height of its crest and reared its head and stretched its broad shoulders out across the firmament, it caught Orion's prowling eye. The hunter bent his bow and loosed. The missile hurled forth, exploding from the taut string like matter rejoicing in the moment of creation; it leaped through the unfathomed gaps between stars, ebullient, sizzle-hot, a feast of gases and fire, singing through the spaces between spaces, crackling and whistling in its song, racing across the arc of time, flashing through aeonian marvels and towering nebulae, fierce and bright as the dawn in its course until, in the blink of an eye, it smote the mountain. The monolithic left shoulder of the ridge, pierced by the star-stroke, dropped heavily and the concussion of the blow rollicked over the Appalachians like a scream. Orion frowned, for his missile had not struck the heart, and his eye drifted on in search of other prey. The wounded shoulder lay open to the sky, a vast gaping hollow, and the mountain swept onward, carried forward through oceans of time in its long, patient journey to the shore.

Though Adams was suspicious from the beginning, it was not immediately apparent to Colonel Bead that something was wrong. The six-day journey to the Cumberland Mountain garrison had tired him considerably and his mind was bent toward arrival, welcome, and the enjoyment of a warm bed. When the road began to narrow, Adams worried that they had taken a wrong turn, but Colonel Bead trod on. When they came to the remains of a weeks-dead Confederate soldier lying scavenged on the roadside, Adams assumed Union encroachment, but Colonel Bead judged it no more than misfortune. When they came to the crest of a ridge and looked down into a broad, circular bowl of land that stretched between them and the Cumberland Mountain garrison on the other side, Adams had an uneasy feeling about the crater-like valley and suggested they go around it. But Colonel Bead paid him no mind, and through the valley they went.

As they descended into the hollow, the road became so narrow that it vanished altogether among weeds and fallen logs and strange conical stones strewn across the ground. They found it again only by faithfully maintaining their heading until the path emerged once more from the brush. At length, the land began to slope upward and Colonel Bead's spirits rose with it, for he knew that at the crest of the ridge ahead his new garrison awaited, and within it lay the promise of peace and quiet. Adams followed closely behind, but he suspected some unseen foil to his colonel's hopes. To Colonel Bead's great perturbation, Adams was right.

Pop-smack-sizzle. A flurry of splinters erupted from a hickory tree three feet to Colonel Bead's right side. While Adams threw himself to the ground and covered his head with his hands, Colonel Bead turned and inspected the tree curiously as if it had exploded at him in some sort of arboreal insult. He ran his fingers across the grey bark and then used the tip of his index finger to gently test the sharpness of a splinter jutting out of the tree's shattered sapwood.

"Suh, hide you-uh-self!"

Colonel Bead dug into the tree's soft, exposed flesh with his fingernail and scratched at the warm metal of an impacted musket ball.

"Would you look at that, Adams? They've shot at us."

"I puh-ray they don't shoot again, suh. I beg you get down."

Colonel Bead turned away from the tree and looked up the hill toward the garrison. "They've mistaken us for Union scouts, I expect. Come on, Adams."

Adams stayed put while Colonel Bead went on. After he had taken three steps—*pop-smack-sizzle*—another innocent hickory exploded. Adams said, "Day-um!" and pulled his pistol out and looked around for something to shoot.

"Lay down your arms and surrender!" A young blue-capped Union soldier raised his head above a redoubt some thirty yards further up the hill and pointed his musket at Adams. Adams dropped his pistol into the dirt and raised his hands in the air to show he meant it. Colonel Bead observed all this with growing confusion.

"Get on the ground," cried the Union soldier. "I'll shoot you."

"How did he get up there, Adams?" said Colonel Bead. He slumped to his knees and and looked from Adams to the soldier ponderously. "Quiet!" The young soldier stood from behind the redoubt and walked toward them with his musket shouldered. He narrowed one eye and sighted down the gunbarrel, laying a sure aim on Colonel Bead. "I got me a colonel!" he yelled. The heads of three more soldiers sprouted from the redoubt and peered down the hill like curious rabbits. "I seen him first. I seen 'em both."

"Can I have one of them?" said one of the sprouts.

"You think they got any more?" said another.

"They-uh ah but two of us," said Adams.

"What did he say?"

"He said they wasn't but two."

"I seen 'em first," said the musket-wielding soldier as he kicked Adams' pistol out of reach. "They both of them mine. Get up."

Adams stood up and kept his hands in the air.

Colonel Bead nodded pleasantly and spoke as if he intended to settle the dispute with weapons of manners and hospitality. "I am a colonel of the Army of Tennessee, and I should like to speak with the garrison commander. There's no need to bring the war out here. Let's all sit down at the mess tent and have a cup of coffee. How does that sound?"

The sprouts looked at one another in silence, then at the soldier in the road, then back at the colonel. "That old man crazy," one of them said.

"A fine idea, colonel. Let's go on up to the garrison and have some coffee. You lead on." The soldier with the musket smirked and stepped behind the colonel and Adams and waited.

"That wasn't so bad was it, Adams?"

Adams sighed and shook his head. "No, suh."

When he passed under the Union flag raised over the gate of the Cumberland Mountain garrison, Colonel Bead's confusion began to clear. When he was marched past the mess tent without any offer of hospitality, he began to doubt that coffee was forthcoming. When his subsequent questions and demands went unanswered and laughed-at, he began to feel indignant. But when he was pushed unceremoniously into a fenced kennel furnished only with a lean-to, a fire pit, and an uncouth bucket, he finally began to understand that he had become a prisoner of war. In fact, the Union had dislodged the Army of Tennessee from the garrison only a few weeks before, news of which would either trouble or amuse General Felix Zollicoffer when he found out—Colonel Bead wasn't sure which. He took some comfort, however, in the fact that he had maintained the company of Lieutenant Adams in this new trial—though this provided little comfort to Adams himself, who preferred to have been shot.

Within their kennel, they discovered three other men huddled beneath the lean-to. There seemed nothing human about them save their eyes, which stood out from their emaciated faces like fat grubs in rotten wood. Faint clouds of vapor puffed from each of six withered nostrils. The grey tatters of their Confederate uniforms hung from their limbs like grave-wrappings.

Colonel Bead knelt in front of the three wasted men and looked into their unseeing eyes. He touched one of the six knobby knees and shook it gently, but it only clattered against the other like a dried branch swayed by the wind. "Hello, I say. Are you boys here long?" No glimmer of recognition or conscious thought stirred their silence, and the six eyes held to their sightless stare.

"What's happened to them, suh?"

The colonel frowned and tenderly touched one of the wasted cheeks. A corps badge dangled from the shoulder of the boy's uniform, and Colonel

Bead tugged it free and rubbed it between his fingers thoughtfully. "They are poor boys who should have gone to the sea, Adams. They should have followed a star."

Twice each day, a guard threw a handful of hardtack over the fence and dropped a bucket of watery broth at the gate so they could sop the hardtack in it and eat. Adams saw that the three "scarecrows," as he called them, did not move even for food, and Colonel Bead tried to feed them by force but withdrew in defeat. The scarecrows never stirred and never ceased in their wide-eyed watch, and after the third week of their captivity, neither Colonel Bead nor Adams could account for the life that maintained them; they neither ate nor drank, and yet the vapor of their breath in the cold air never changed: it neither quickened nor slowed, but only went on steadily and without purpose like the silent gaze of their protuberant eyes.

"It's unnatural, suh."

"Is it?" asked Colonel Bead.

"No man can live without food or wat-ah."

"Who's to say what's natural, Adams? I can never tell. My father once told me that there are corners of the ocean where fish leap out of the water, flapping their fins like wings, and they soar into the sky and sing like birds. I told him that it sounded strange but he said it was the most natural thing in the world. What do you think, Adams?"

"I don't know, suh."

"I don't either. But I'd like to. Sometimes I think there's too much to know and more to see than any man can ever manage, and it doesn't seem fair somehow. Maybe that's why the scarecrows stare, Adams. Maybe they've got it right. Maybe they see everything, everything there is—and they can't bear even to blink for they'll miss the best part and break the spell and never get to the end of it all. Maybe that's it, Adams. Move out of the way. Let them see."

Adams moved aside, and Colonel Bead sat down beside the scarecrows and drew up his knees like one of them and looked where they looked. He stared for a long time but saw only the kennel's fence before him and the

Union guards beyond and the grey mountain looming in the distance. He joined in the endless watch until his eyelids grew heavy and he slept.

When morning came, Adams stood at the kennel gate and shouted. He demanded more and better food. He demanded clean water. He jumped up and down and cried for warmer blankets. He cursed every Union soldier he saw and spat at them until they moved out of spittle-range. He screamed for paper and pen and the chance to write to his wife and children. He spewed and roared and growled until Colonel Bead entreated him to come away and be calm.

"It's beastly, Adams. Be a gentleman. The war won't last. We've only to abide it while it does."

Adams tried to say "Yes, suh," but he'd undone his voice and only made a gurgling sound.

"Did I ever tell you that my father was a prisoner, Adams? He said he fell afoul of pirates once and they sold him off to the owner of an Antarctic diamond mine. He took great pride in the fact that he was sold for twice the sum of his fellow prisoners owing to his strong arms, his resilience in extreme cold, and his ability to see in the dark like a cat—all of which made him perfect for Antarctic mining. He said that for two years he never saw the sun except as it shone in the diamonds he found, for an Antarctic diamond catches starlight no matter where it is and shines out even in complete darkness. Did you know that, Adams?"

Adams gurgled and raised a doubtful eyebrow.

"He was stuck in that mine so long he forgot what warmth felt like. His right hand froze solid and he used it for a rock hammer to beat gems out of the earth, and the jewels he hewed out were wonders of the world. He uncovered a diamond the size of a human head. It lit up the whole mine like the sun had risen in the deeps of it." Adams nodded his head dutifully. "He couldn't keep what he found, of course, which was terrible unfortunate for my mother. But in time his captain did free him. She refitted the *Esprit de la Mer* for ice-breaking, which was why she had to leave him so long in the mine. He said the ship arrived like a battering ram smashing the ice and shattering it like china glass. His red-haired captain played a fiddle tune that put the guards to sleep and she stole away with my father and all his fellows." Colonel Bead paused and sighed and looked up at the mountain. "Wouldn't that be something, Adams? To be stolen away?"

Adams nodded and smiled at the colonel as one does at a grandparent who no longer understands the present and instead retreats into the familiar company of the past. That night the colonel sat again beside the scarecrows and joined them in their watch until he slept.

The autumn air crisped and nipped, and every day it licked harder at the colonel's ears and nose. His captors paid him no more mind than a stray dog, and as the temperature plumbed lower and lower depths, Adams cried out for firewood and coffee and blankets and hot bacon and daily newspapers and cards. Adams yelled for three straight days until a Union sergeant threw him a charred log and made him beg for an ember with which to kindle it. Adams tenderly blew on the ember and coaxed it to life, and he and Colonel Bead gathered around the single ruby–hued gem of warmth and thawed themselves as thankfully as if they were gathered at the burning bush of Moses. Thereafter, a guard delivered a single log and a glowing ember each day, and Adams treated them each as if they were treasures of unspeakable price.

Each morning, the colonel inspected the scarecrows. He snapped his fingers at them and waved his hand in front of their faces. He whispered into their ears and slipped his hand into their shirts to feel the beating of their hearts. They abided his investigations without protest or reflex and maintained their unblinking stare into space. Each day, the colonel sat with them longer and longer. He assumed their posture, drawing up his knees and slumping his head forward like a buzzard and peeling his eyes wide to stare into the distance and see what they saw.

"Come and watch with us, Adams," said Colonel Bead as he sidled up next to the outermost scarecrow. "The yelling and carrying on will do no good. Come and watch."

Adams' lip turned up in abhorrence. "No, suh. It isn't natural." As he looked at the colonel he saw that he could no longer easily tell his commanding officer apart from the other scarecrows. His face had thinned in captivity and his uniform was worn thin; soon it would be in tatters. When the colonel assumed the position of his watch, he seemed only a degree or two more lively than the withering creatures beside him. But Adams said nothing more and did not protest the colonel's watch. Instead he removed the buckle of his belt and began to scrape at the base of the gatepost.

Colonel Bead awoke in the night. An eerie howl of wind startled him and he jerked upright. At his side, the scarecrows watched, their breaths puffing in quiet white billows. Adams leaned against the gatepost, snoring. The colonel crossed his arms and rubbed his shoulders. He chattered his terrible teeth and blinked the sleep from his eyes. He leaned his head back and wondered how close was morning, and then he looked up into the Gap and saw a mist pour through it and gather up into a cloud that flowed and swirled like a gossamer gown. Beneath the hem of the gown a white sheet of rain descended and froze the earth wherever it fell. In the moonlight the sheeting rain looked to Colonel Bead like an ivory foot moving surely and indifferently beneath a cloudy raiment. The heel pressed into the trees of the Cumberland Gap and rocked forward as the toes settled onto the vales and fingers of the mountain pass and iced them in white crystal. A freezing gale blew across the garrison, and Colonel Bead shivered and watched with the scarecrows and dared not blink, and he saw what few men ever have: the coming of the White Lady. She stepped down out of the sky, descending slowly, her movements imperceptible to anyone not trained to look long and hard into the smooth, calculated precision of her advance. But Colonel Bead had learned to see and he watched with unblinking eyes. She lit upon the earth as a young girl slips out of her bed and onto the cold floor. She covered the treetops and Appalachian balds in her cottony robe and draped her lace across the valley. As the colonel watched, she raised a gelid finger to her lips and—*ssshhhhhhhh*—her frigid whisper cascaded across the land and swept away the lingering scents and sights of autumn.

When Adams woke the next morning, the ground was covered in snow. He cried for an ember and kindled the fire and turned to wake his colonel but found him un-asleep. Colonel Bead had taken up the stare of the scarecrows in earnest. His jaw hung slack and his eyes were engaged on the mountain.

"Look at me, suh!"

Adams shook Colonel Bead and the colonel's irises pin-wheeled into points. He blinked. "Good morning, Adams." Adams sighed in relief.

"Come to the fi-uh, suh." Adam held out his hand to assist Colonel Bead to his feet, but the colonel turned away. He crawled in front of the scarecrows and stared at them.

"The poor boy," said Colonel Bead. One of the scarecrows had frozen solid. His skin had turned a purple-grey color and his eyes, having seen their last, were closed. Colonel Bead pulled at the boy's arm. "Help me move him by the fire, Adams. We can thaw him."

"No, suh," Adams said.

"Adams, we must. The boy needs help, can't you see?"

Adams pulled the colonel away. "Let him be, suh. I'll see to him." While Colonel Bead rubbed his hands over the meager fire and hummed, Adams dragged the dead man away from his brethren. The boy was frozen stiff, right through to the middle, and Adams had to maneuver the cadaver by degrees. He flipped him end to end, and rolled him, and flopped him, until he upended the poor boy out of sight behind the lean-to.

Four days later Lieutenant Adams and Colonel Bead observed signs of festivity in the heart of the garrison. Though no one informed them directly, the two men deduced from the smell of roasting hams and steaming ciders and the distant sounds of merriment that Christmas had come to the Cumberland Gap. In the late afternoon a Union captain with formidable mustaches presented himself at the gate with a bundle of firewood and a freshly skinned rabbit. He didn't speak, but whether by the illusion of his sharply curled mustaches or by genuine goodwill, he seemed to smile as he delivered his gifts.

"Thank you, captain," said Colonel Bead. The captain haltingly saluted the colonel and departed without breaking his silence.

Adams prepared the feast and the two men ate. Adams tried to engage Colonel Bead in a Christmas carol, but the colonel turned aside his attempts and stared nervously at the mountain pass as evening fell.

"Would you some mo-uh rabbit, suh?" Adams tore off a haunch and held it out in expectation. Colonel Bead waved it off, parrying the leg of beast as surely as an enemy's blow. Adams spat into the fire. He put the rabbit leg into his mouth, clapped his lips over it, and pulled the bone out clean.

As Adams squatted beside the fire and chewed his game, Colonel Bead drew his coat close around him. He took his seat beside the scarecrows and looked out beyond the firelight into the darkness. Adams turned away and reached for the last of the rabbit, and when he turned back, three scarecrows stared at him, not two. The colonel had blended into their number completely.

"Colonel Bead, suh?"

The colonel did not answer.

"*Colonel Bead*, suh?" Adams frowned and rubbed his neck and chewed his rabbit ponderously. Then he slipped out his belt buckle and sat down beside the gatepost. While Union soldiers filled the tents and shanty buildings with the merry notes of Christmas, the only sound outside in the biting cold was the *scrape, scrape, scrape* of brass against wood.

When the sun came up, there was a new fall of snow on the ground and the second scarecrow had turned into an ice block. He was frozen through like the first and had a thick spike of ice hanging down from his nose. The spike had grown so long that it had frozen to the ground between the scarecrow's legs. He looked very like a crystal statue of an elephantine Hindu diety that Adams had once seen in a shop window in Atlanta. Adams stared at the spectacle in bewilderment and chose not to bother chipping him free of the ground to roll him out of sight. Instead, Adams knelt in front of Colonel Bead. The withered man stared through him.

"Colonel?" Adams took the colonel by the shoulders and shook him but his stare didn't waver. Adams shook him harder and still the old man stared. Adams took his belt buckle in one hand and Colonel Bead's arm in the other. He put the ragged metal edge of the buckle against the cold white skin of the

forearm. "I am sorry, suh." He drew the metal across the colonel's skin, opening a cut an inch long. A viscous bead of blood seeped out of the wound.

"Adams?"

"Yes, suh."

"My arm hurts, Adams."

"Yes, suh. It's but a scratch, suh."

"What's that, Adams?"

"Come to the fi-uh, suh."

"The fire?"

"Yes, suh."

The colonel broke free of the scarecrow's watch and crawled to the fire.
Adams sat beside him and leaned his body against his colonel's and rubbed
his arms and legs. "Tell me a story about you-uh fath-uh, suh. Tell me about
the sea."

"The sea?"

"Yes, suh."

"The sea. The sea. I scarcely remember it, Adams. You must go to see it
someday."

"Yes, suh. I will, suh. Warm you-uh hands at the fi-uh, colonel. It's warm,
see?" Adams pulled Colonel Bead's hands from his lap and pushed them
toward the flame. "Like so, colonel." He showed the colonel how to rub his
hands together and hold them close enough to the fire to thaw. The colonel's
glassy eyes wheeled into focus and his mind warmed as his hands did. He
became himself again.

"Thank you, Adams." The old man's face flushed with a tinge of shame.

"Yes, suh." When he was satisfied that the colonel was in possession of his
wits, Adams moved to the gatepost. *Scrape-scrape-scrape.*

Colonel Bead huddled by the fire and clapped his hands for warmth
and muttered to himself. "She's seen me. She's coming. She's coming over the
mountain. Never should have left the sea." He nodded to himself and continued his muttering and often turned to look at the single remaining scarecrow.
"Do you see her?" he'd ask. He'd wait for an answer but when none came he'd

turn back to the fire and clap his hands and moan and fall into indistinct murmurs that Adams could not make out. *Scrape-scrape-scrape.*

There was no firewood that day, and no broth, nor any bread, and no soldier stirred in the garrison. Adams laid the leftover bones of the previous day's rabbit in the embers of the fire until they were brittle. He ate what he could and ground the rest to meal in his mouth. He fed the meal to Colonel Bead who could not have managed the bones with his awful teeth. Neither man spoke to the other and they watched the last gleam of the ruby embers fade away in chilling silence.

"She'll come, Adams."

"Who will, suh?"

"Watch for her. Come sit with me." Colonel Bead crawled to the scarecrow's side and assumed the position of the watch.

"No, suh. Come away from they-uh."

"I saw her, Adams. I saw her."

"Colonel, we ah leaving." Adams walked to the gate. He looked through the fence and listened. There was no movement in the garrison, and no sound. With one swift kick of his boot, the base of the gatepost snapped where he had nearly sawn through it with his buckle. "Come, colonel. Let's go."

"What?"

Adams pulled Colonel Bead up by the arm and dragged him toward the gate.

"It's no use, Adams. What are you doing?"

Adams pulled the gatepost upward, creating a gap of about a foot under the bottom wire of the fence. "Und-uh, colonel."

Colonel Bead sputtered in confusion, but he obeyed. He wriggled under the wire and once on the other side he stood up and looked in bafflement at Adams as he scuffled under the fence like a panicked animal. Adams leaped to his feet and crouched over, ready to run. His eyes darted across the garrison, inspecting each shadow and corner for any eyes that might have spotted them. He grabbed Colonel Bead by the arm and rushed through the unbroken snow to the corner of the nearest tent. As Adams looked around the edge of the tent toward the garrison's gate, Colonel Bead looked behind them. They'd disturbed a wide trench of snow and it led the colonel's eyes back to the kennel gate; just beyond it he could see the scarecrow staring at him.

"The poor boy should have followed a star."

Adams jerked the colonel's arm and they ran toward the garrison's main entry. Icy wind howled in the treetops and a fresh snow began to fall. Adams pulled up short and leaned against a dead tree. He looked around madly for signs of pursuit, but nothing moved in the camp. There was no campfire lit, no light in any tent, no hint of distant conversation or laughter. Only the mournful keening of the wind filled the empty space of the garrison.

"Good God," said Colonel Bead. Adams turned toward the colonel sharply, his eyes alert. The colonel put out his hand and stroked the dead tree beside Adams' face. "The poor boy," he muttered. Adams stepped back in horror. A Union soldier stood upright beside him, caught firmly in the position of attention where the winter had frozen him to the ground. Adams backed away and looked around the courtyard. It wasn't empty. He had failed to see it clearly. It was a crowd of activity that had been stopped, seized, and held captive by the sudden advent of winter. Men stood at their posts, hard as brick, covered in snow and long, sharp sickles of ice. Some were frozen with their rifles shouldered, the barrels jutting up like dead branches in the wind. Others had been arrested in moments of laughter, heads thrown back, mouths open, teeth glimmering under layers of ice. One man sat atop his warhorse; he had drawn his sword and pointed it up at the mountain pass as if he had seen his enemy and ordered a last desperate charge—but before his moment of glory, he'd been caught and enshrined like a memorial.

Adams stumbled backward, eyes wide. The courtyard had become a statuary of horrors. He grabbed Colonel Bead and dragged him through the garrison gate. The wind whistled across the Stars and Stripes and they also were held captive, frozen mid-flap in the grip of the White Lady.

The colonel stumbled behind Adams as they ran. A deep blanket of snow covered the road and they had to stop every fifty yards to examine the surrounding trees and gauge the lay of the road between them. The wind screamed.

"Do you hear it?" Colonel Bead shouted.

Adams ignored him. He dragged his colonel blindly into the crater-like valley before the garrison. When he stopped, he looked up the slope behind them, still suspicious of pursuit, then turned back and spotted the place they'd been captured. The snow was heaped up against the redoubt and three soldiers stared at them. They were frozen in the act of rising as if, having heard the approach of some unimaginable calamity, they had stood to meet it and had been entombed in the instant of its revelation. Adams ran, stubbornly hauling Colonel Bead in tow. When they reached the trough of the valley, Colonel Bead stumbled and fell.

"Get up, suh. Get up!"

"Where's the road, Adams? Do you see it?"

Barren trees studded the land around them. The ice-sheathed trunks stabbed into the air, dark and withered and evenly spaced, giving them no sign at all of a well-traveled road. The line of their trail through the snow curled down from the northern rise and ended abruptly at Colonel Bead's feet like a question mark.

"Do you hear that, Adams?"

Adams ran forward. He kicked at the snow bank. He dug and burrowed and struck the weed-covered ground and cursed. He ran to the right and cleared the snow again. "Find the road, colonel!" He spun and ran and burrowed again, finding only rock and frozen brush beneath the snow.

Colonel Bead watched Adams' commotion in wonder and began to laugh. "We've got off it, Adams. We've got off it at last!" Then the colonel too began to kick at the snow and shovel it with his hands. He smiled like a boy tearing into a long-awaited gift. He flung snow right and left. He beat at it and tore at it and hurled it away from him and laughed. Then he stopped abruptly and stared at the ground. He bent over and picked up a small conical stone and turned it in his fingers.

"She's coming, Adams." The colonel tossed the strange stone to Adams and looked up at the horizon. "I told you I could hear it."

The wind squalled around them, pulling the snow from the sky and lashing their skin, raking them with a million tiny blades. Adams inspected the stone. It fit easily into the palm of his hand and was formed by hundreds of v-shaped radiations originating at one end and spreading out along its length. It looked like rays of light fossilized and held captive in cold stone. "What is it, suh?" yelled Adams. The icy gale tore his words from his mouth and hurled them into the distance.

"It's a shatter-cone."

"A what, suh?"

"It means we've followed the right road, Adams. And we've arrived. Don't you hear it?" Colonel Bead smiled and tilted his ear to the eastern horizon.

"Day-um it, suh! We will die out he-uh!" Adams hurled the stone into the wind and the wind whispered to him—*ssssshhhhhhhh*! He saw a tower rise up in the Gap of the mountain, a misty column of vapor that swirled and danced like a woman robed in silk. Then for a moment the wind stuttered in the air. It slackened and swirled as if it had met with some immovable force through which it could not pass and could only go around. In that instant, Adams heard something that sounded like a note. He looked at Colonel Bead, who raised an eyebrow and grinned. The wind eddied again, creating a momentary calm in which Colonel Bead and Lieutenant Adams were free of cold and wind and noise and were shrouded instead by the bright warmth of music.

When the eddy passed, Colonel Bead's face broke into a shape that he could not remember ever having formed before. It was a smile of purest delight, a smile that breaks only upon those who have looked long and, having looked, have learned at last to see.

From the east, the Appalachian Mountains heaved up against the clouds. The winter wind drove against them, covering them in white water and sending it spraying over the caps of the high peaks in great plumes. Amid the violence of the storm, a tall white form rose above the saddle between two crags. It was a sail. Its mast tilted and swayed and climbed upward until Colonel Bead and Lieutenant Adams could see a fair white ship at the crest of the ridge. It tottered on the ledge as its sails luffed. Its lines screamed in the gale. Then it seemed that something in the nature of the ship pushed back against the wind. The sails punched full. Colonel Bead and Lieutenant Adams heard again a sharp, playful measure of music sweep past and the ship began to tilt. With an illusory sluggishness the ship rocked forward onto the face of the mountain and descended along its curve. It rushed earthward like the calving of a glacier and vanished momentarily into the valley before exploding up the slope of the opposite ridge and leaping into the air, barely able to contain the power that drove it. Music was everywhere. It filled the sails of the ship's main, mizzen, and foremasts, each set with its full complement of cloth, as the vessel thundered across the mountain steeps.

"I told you she would come, Adams."

Adams had no reply. He stared dumbfounded while the ship altered its tack and turned toward them.

"Are you ready to go?" asked Colonel Bead.

"Whey-uh ah we going, suh?"

Colonel Bead smiled as the ship slipped gracefully down into the crater-valley. The sounds of fiddle music filled the air, and though he could see the fury of the White Lady raging in the Gap, the crater was calm and warm and peaceful. The ship slowed and a man stepped to the rail. He cast a rope down, which landed at Adams' feet.

"After you, lieutenant," said Colonel Bead.

Adams, still slack-jawed, took hold of the rope, and the crew hauled him aboard. When the rope was thrown back out for Colonel Bead, he took hold of it fiercely and looked up. The man at the rail smiled as he hauled Barnabas aboard. From behind his smile, a single bright tooth twinkled and shone.

"Hold fast!" cried the bright-toothed man.

The air around the ship exploded with music. Colonel Bead turned and saw a woman at the helm whose hair shimmered and rippled like flames. She held a golden fiddle in the cleft of her neck. Beside her a tall man with a thin beard and a kind face smiled at her as he watched her play. He looked up at the sails, then across the starboard rail at the raging storm issuing through the Gap.

"Play well, *cherie*," he said, then turned away and shouted to the crew. "Get underway. Prepare to tack. Lay a course three degrees east of the Pleiades. Rough sea ahead, gentlemen. Ready yourselves."

The great ship heaved over. Music filled the sails and drove them. Colonel Bead stepped to the rail and looked down. Below him he spotted the well-trodden road. The ship turned away from it and gathered speed and fled the valley as the White Lady howled in their wake. Colonel Barnabas Bead did not look down again.

ANOTHER WORLD
by Chris Yokel

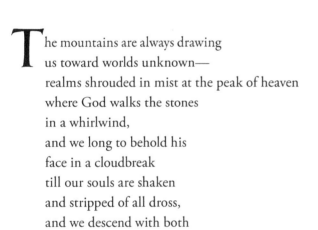

The mountains are always drawing
us toward worlds unknown—
realms shrouded in mist at the peak of heaven
where God walks the stones
in a whirlwind,
and we long to behold his
face in a cloudbreak
till our souls are shaken
and stripped of all dross,
and we descend with both
a little less, and
a little more than who we were.

Fact: That's not Teddy Roosevelt on Mount Rushmore; it's Ron Block.

THE BLACK HORIZON (PART IV)
Story and Illustrations by Jamin Still

THE BLACK HORIZON

I've gone for weeks without seeing a soul, feeling nothing but the roll of the waves and the breeze on my face as I sail toward the setting sun. Anticipation has been building. I sighted The Sparrows, where I had calculated they would be, the last lonely islands of the West. Some might have stopped there, content with reaching that all but unreachable place, but I knew that The Sparrows were just the beginning: the Greatest Adventure was still before me. I took to the quickening waters, leaving the last island behind, and aimed my prow toward the Darkness. After The Sparrows I didn't even need to hoist sail. But I did anyway, to hasten my journey.

How I've longed for The Black Horizon and The Falls! I don't know much about them (who does?), but the longing is in my blood, in my bones, it even creeps into my dreams. I've been waiting so long for this, fearing it, but needing it. It's the Greatest Adventure. The Horizon is there, beckoning, drawing me, whispering to me.

Tomorrow, if my calculations are correct, I will reach it and then—The Falls.

—The Final Journal Entry of Jacob Hardcastle

Fact: When Jamin Still writes his autobiography, he intends to call it *Jamin Still Life*.

THE DISTANCE
by Russ Ramsey

"Do you who live in radiance
hear the prayers of those of us who live in skin?
We have a love that's not as patient as yours was.
Still, we do love now and then."[1]

       – Rich Mullins

I didn't anticipate this distance I feel. Distance from others. From God.

I am at home now, tethered to a fanny pack that holds a machine that pumps IV antibiotics directly into my heart through a catheter in my arm. There is a drawer in my refrigerator full of very expensive medicine. On my dining table sits a red tray with a large box of sterile latex gloves, alcohol swabs, and syringes of saline solution used to flush the PICC line when I change my medications.

The pump runs twenty-four hours a day. I can feel the medicine in my blood. I ran the numbers. In the two weeks since I was first admitted to the hospital, I have had over six gallons of syrupy antibiotics pumped into my system. I feel syrupy and sluggish.

---

[1] Rich Mullins "Hard to Get," from the album *The Jesus Record*, Myrrh Records, 1998

Once the IV treatments have killed all the bacteria and my blood tests come back clean, we will schedule open-heart surgery. My surgeon tells me this must be done as soon as possible.

I cannot remember what it feels like to be well. This is not so much a complaint as an observation. Like a frog in a pot, over time I've grown accustomed to the effects of my infection—the night sweats, the constant chill, my foggy mind, the ache when I stand up, my general malaise.

I have a recurring dream from which I wake with a start. In the dream I am being chased and I am afraid, but that is all I can ever recall. I wake trembling with fear. It takes a few minutes to remember where I am and shake it off. When I lay back down, my pillow is drenched in cold sweat. I go through this routine alone almost every night. I do not wake my wife and I don't think to talk about it during the day. I am the only one who knows that every night when everyone else in the house is sound asleep, I am frightened awake. Whether it be the hound of heaven or the devils of hell, this is my nightmare. It has become part of the rhythm of my day. It happens so often that it feels normal.

The fever has given me an ashen complexion. My friends tell me I look gray. They are deeply concerned when they say it. I hear it in the ways they choose their words. They want to say the right thing but don't know what that is, so sometimes they say the wrong thing. I understand. I say the wrong things too. Sometimes I make little jokes about dying.

There is a strange relational order to this experience. I feel a great burden to care for loved ones who, themselves, are afraid for me. I do not know what hounds are chasing them in secret, but I see the fear in their eyes when they ask me to tell them my story. So I try to tell it in a way that will comfort them. I want to reassure them that I will be fine. But I do not know if that is true.

Nevertheless, I, the infirm, find myself caring for the sorrows and fears of the well. I do not resent them for this; not even a little. I love my friends. I want to comfort them. I am a pastor. Caring for the hearts of others is part of my profession. But walking through affliction is a work that is bound by limitation. Often it isn't that the afflicted are unwilling to let others in. It is just that there comes a certain point in a person's suffering where there is no apparent port of entry.

I saw this inaccessibility in these words written by a friend of mine who recently lost a child. In the rawness of his grief, he wrote to me: "It has been almost thirty-six hours since I held my dead son and cried out to my God for the miracle of life. I held his head in my arms and covered his face with my tears. With each breath I breathed his hair into my mouth. I wanted to consume him, and swallow death, and see him live."

This walk through suffering follows a lonesome road. I wanted to do for my friend's sorrow what he wanted to do for his son's death; I wanted to consume it. But that was not mine to do. I could venture only so far into his pain before I could go no further. The precious words he sent were his way of coming out to meet me.

My suffering is not so severe as his. Still, I do sense a distance between myself and those I love. To close this gap, I have to come out of my present distress to meet them just as they have to step in to a suffering that is not their own to meet me. If I wanted, I suppose I could withdraw from people on the basis that they don't understand my pain. And in a sense I would be right. But what sort of fool would require such a thing of those who only want to love me?

My affliction has provided something people rarely possess—objective data that my heart is failing. But in truth, my position is really no different from anyone else's—not when it comes to the question of our mortality. The only real difference between us is that certain pieces of information about my current position in this world are known. But no one is promised tomorrow. Some of the very people who are afraid of losing me might well be taken from this world long before I go.

Still, the data about my condition leads to a sense of distance. It is a distance born out of love and concern. And fear. But it remains a distance—one I suspect has been here all along, but has now stepped into a light by which it may be seen. The fear of losing me has illuminated the truth that no one has any power to keep me. Though there are hounds in the shadows bearing down on us all, we have caught a glimpse of one of mine.

I wish I could take away their fear. Here is that strange relational order again. I see people trying to imagine being in my position. They say this must be very difficult for me. Then I do the same with them. I imagine how sad they must feel worrying about someone they love. That must be difficult for them.

In truth, I do know what they are feeling. I feel it whenever I think about my friend Barbara. Barbara and I have been in a fellowship group together for four years. Our families are intertwined.

Barbara is one of the living ones—a saint with a blue streak. She has that rare ability to get things done quickly while making those around her feel like she has all the time in the world for them. She is a woman who has many friends who all count her as their best friend, and none of them are mistaken. Full of grace and moxie, the Lord is with her.

Barbara is battling cancer. She has been in this fight for over five years. She lives her life snapping back and forth between progress and set-backs— her husband, children, and friends snapping with her. I am one of those friends. We struggle with her disease, though she works hard to lead us well. But because we are not her, no matter how close we would like to be, we have no choice but to watch her suffering from a distance.

It is hard for her to go through. It is hard for us to watch.

—⁊⁊⁊—

Like Barbara, I have now become a prayer request.

More people than I can count have told me they are praying for my family and me. I am touched by the idea that we are so greatly loved from such a distance. When people who have been praying for me come to see me, they hope for news that their prayers are being answered. I try to measure my words to encourage their faith.

"I'm better than I was," I say. "My doctors assure me I'll be fine."

I try to be my normal self. But there is a PICC line in my arm and a fanny pack around my waist with a machine that makes a little ticking noise as it pumps its syrup into my heart. So there is a distance.

I tire easily. I don't have much strength. I find myself sitting down while everyone else is standing. They now must look down on me.

"I'm better than I was."

—∾—

Prayer is more complicated than it used to be. It isn't that I have trouble praying or doubt that God hears me. I don't on either count. It's that I don't know what God has in mind for me. When I pray, as Jesus taught his disciples, "not my will, but yours be done," I feel that the stakes are somehow suddenly higher, even though I know on an intellectual level that it is an error to think that the stakes have ever been lower.

My prayers now feel more like an exercise in surrender than a conversation. For most of my life I have prayed to a God I believe made and sustains the universe. I have always believed him to be good. But now my faith requires me to entertain the question of whether I can say with Job, "though he slay me, I will hope in him."[2]

I think I can, if he helps me. But I am aware in new ways that the God I believe in is not one to keep us from affliction. Rather, he is one who works through it. His ways are not my ways and his thoughts are not my thoughts.[3] If I take the position that something must make sense to me if I am to believe it makes any sense at all, can I still call myself a man of faith—one who believes in what cannot be known and hopes in what is unseen? What sort of faith could I honestly claim if I required the God I believed in to only do what made sense to this earthbound creature?

Here again is distance. His ways are not my ways and his thoughts are not my thoughts.

---

[2] Job 13:15
[3] Isaiah 55:8

These days my prayers are filled with things I do not understand, and they are spoken to a God I do not understand. Surely the same must be true for those who are praying for me.

—※—

I realize I have a choice about how I will regard this distance. I have a choice in how I respond to people when they say the wrong thing or avoid me because they don't know what to say. The lines have fallen for us all in strange places. Who knows what the rules of engagement are? I don't want to become so self-important that I require a certain kind of elegance from those who cannot help but stumble around this unfamiliar stage.

It serves no purpose for me to be touchy about how people interact with me or I with them. We live most of our days avoiding the subject of our mortality. It takes courage to face death, and trying to be brave is the same as being brave.

The truth is, I don't always know how to be. If I encourage people to take a casual approach toward my affliction, am I robbing them of the opportunity to express what they really feel? If I treat my situation with utmost solemnity, am I being unnecessarily morbid?

I talked with Barbara about this. She told me about how when her hair started to fall out after her first round of chemotherapy, she and her daughters went into their back yard where she shook and rubbed her head until there were no loose hairs left. She said it looked like a ginger snow as her red hair just kept falling and falling. They cried at first, until they burst into laughter. It was both tragic and comic.

In affliction we cry and then we laugh. Or we laugh and then we cry. We become schooled in the art of being able to feel more than one thing at a time. Since the afflicted live among the well, moments like these are bound to come. And with them, this feeling of distance.

But it does not need to be a separating distance. Just as I must not demand that I understand everything God is doing in order to pray to him,

I cannot expect others to understand everything I am experiencing in order for them to talk to me. The distance is real. The least I can do is come out to meet those who seek me. Like a docent in a museum, I can try to explain what they are seeing. I can try to help.

I am the steward of this sacred distance. But since it is something I cannot erase, I shall become its curator instead.

Fact: Russ Ramsey is the *real* star of the TV show *Nashville*.

PROCESSIONAL
by Jen Rose Yokel

We make a clumsy march, these machines
gleaming in the winter sun,
a line of old sedans,
hulking SUVs,
and dirt-crusted trucks.

And the leader of our patched-up parade,
long, stern, and black
plods on

led and followed
by flashing lights.

"There was a time when people pulled over,"
		Dad says,
and on the two-lane back roads
they still do.

Work trucks, like beasts of burden,
and old beaters with fading paint jobs
slide over and stop
where the dust blows up,
scatters,
settles,
marking us all.

GHOSTS OF VISBY
by Andrew Peterson

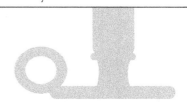

W hen I walk the streets of Visby—

Old Visby with its skeletal ruins,
Twisting streets, and narrow alleys
Arched with stone gateways
And carriage roads—

I am dimly aware of the ghosts
Of the last thousand years,
Jostled and jubilant as they pass
Each other, and me.

But I find, the more I walk here,
The more I come to know
The location of my hotel, the café,
The old church, and the coffee shop
Where I write this,

The less I sense their spectral
Presence, and so I turn instead
To imagination, where the millennia merge
And time is a small inconvenience,
Nothing more.

There, I do the haunting.

CANDLEWOOD
by Lanier Ivester

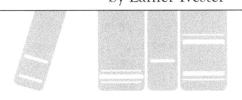

September 29, 20—

Esteemed Companion,

It is with the utmost solicitude that I take my pen in hand to enquire after your health, trusting that the cheerful hopes long lodged in the heart of an admiring friend will not be disappointed, and that soon I shall receive the happy news of this letter finding you in the very prime of happiness. I shall be glad to hear that the neuralgia has abated, as do all other such complaints which try the soul in this degenerate age, and that you have thus been restored to the round of duties most dear to your domestic soul.

Isn't that a scream? I lifted it from an old letter I found in the attic. Yes, my dear, this house has everything—even boxes of crumbling missives languishing under the eaves. I told Sam that I could write a hundred books in this place, as long as the ceilings don't drip and the ghosts don't bang around too irreverently in the spaces overhead (to which he replied, man-like, that he thought there might be one spot in the middle of the front parlor that didn't drip and that ghosts were nothing if not irreverent). Between us, I wish I *could* believe in ghosts, for this house would be the perfect place for one. It would make writing a thousand times easier (not to mention more interesting). It's tiresome, you know, having to make everything up out of your own head. *Anyway*, one book would more than excuse this wild experiment of ours. My agent is clean out of patience with the lack of output from this quarter, and Sam (the darling) is at his wit's end with a wife so creatively destitute she can't find two words to rub together. (Have you ever heard of a thirteen-month bout of writer's block? Of course you haven't—you're one of those disgusting souls whose words gush forth in a torrent of unremitting brilliance.) It was all Sam's idea, if you remember—the "period" house, the rural seclusion, the Walter Scott-like immersion in antiquity (if you can call the annals of eastern South Carolina "antiquity")—so if the whole thing fails miserably, I'll still have some shreds of impunity to gather about my starving artist's soul. And if, by some happy accident, I manage to remember how to write—well then, let's hope the wine will justify all this mad stomping of grapes.

And that's where you come in, Sarah-est of Sarahs. I can only imagine your surprise in receiving a hand-written letter, especially from a correspondent so abysmal she can't even keep up with text messages. But those letters in the attic sparked something: perhaps an addressee is what I need, a listener, if you will, to get this engine up and running again. Do you remember the lofty notions we spouted in college about "artists in vacuums"? "A writer without an audience is a blank," we used to say, with all the cheerful sagacity of twenty-one. We talked about the universe sucking the creative life right out of an artist who wasn't communicating with anyone, and how people with no one to say anything to eventually found they had nothing to say. Such a crop of untested ideals—and it's all true, of course. I had an audience once upon a time, thirteen long months ago, but I think I've ceased to believe in them. It's hard enough to sit down at my desk these days (ah, the Resistance!), much less convince myself there is a soul in all the cold world who would give a plug nickel for anything that came out of my head. So here's what I'm proposing: would you consider accepting the burden of a one-sided correspondence? I respect your writing commitments far too much to impose any expectation of a response—it's accountability I'm seeking, not newsy-ness. In return, you shall be excessively diverted every seven days by the lovely inconsequences of my quiet life. Should I fail to deliver (or should you fail to be thoroughly distracted from your work for at least half an hour), you are hereby authorized to compose a series of badly rhymed limericks on the domestic habits of spadefoot toads and publish them in my name.

It just might work, you know. Best case scenario, the craft and discipline of hand-written letters will tune my novelist's tastes to that of an antebellum protagonist. (I know what you're thinking: *If you're already not writing, Robin, go ahead and make it extra fun for yourself by not writing historical fiction.* Trouble is, I'm too stubborn to give up on this series, and I have a heroine on my hands stuck midway between the Panic of 1857 and the attack on Fort Sumter.) Worse case, you'll have a chronicle of my failed experience, which you can then pilfer and paste into a novel of your own and buy a palazzo in Venice on the advance royalties. Fair enough?

All right, now that we've got that settled, I shall proceed to acquaint you with the setting of our little flight of fancy. (Sam's Folly, I like to call it; he prefers Robin's Nest—which I secretly adore.) It really could not be more perfect: the house is reached by a long drive that meanders for about a decade among scrubby live oaks and cedars, with goldenrod and wild asters nodding by the wayside and bobwhites scuttling ahead in the dusty red dirt. Eventually you come upon a broken fence with a broken sign that once said Candlewood, and it's then you can just make out the rust-colored brick of the chimneys poking periscopically above the treetops. One final plunge into a verdant, pine-rimmed basin, occupied by the memory of things primeval, before the trees part like a velvet curtain to reveal a somnolent Low Country house dreaming of its own youth under a canopy of light-laced shadows. The gables are ample and dignified—I've seen some gables in my time that started up out of a rooftop like raised eyebrows, giving the house an air of perpetual surprise, but not so with these. Here are gables that mean to be gables, with plenty of candid-eyed windows without and wide, musty shadows within. There are deep porches on three sides, and a pretty little balcony overlooking the ruin of a garden out back. Heaven only knows what secrets were whispered under that tangled rose arbor on the far side!

Inside, a spacious hall runs the full length of the house (aptly known as a dogtrot, I'm given to understand), dividing the front parlor and library on the left from the dining room and kitchen on the right. Queenie has made it her exclusive domain and trots her little mixed-breed heart out running back and forth to bark at the squirrels in the tangled garden and the jays that venture onto the front porch. It's funny—she won't set a toenail on the staircase (a stately heart pine masterpiece with a newel post the size of a small child), but merely stands at the bottom looking after us with a heartbroken stare when we go up to bed every night. Sam tried to carry her up the first night and she bit him—for the first time in her life. We let her have her way after that, and I placed her bed at the foot of the stairs. She must be more arthritic than we realized.

Sam has claimed the dining room as his studio, as it's got the best light, and a continual incense of oils and varnishes and medium rises from that chamber with a religious consistency. (I wish I had half his discipline.) He's working on a couple of big commissions concurrently: the daughter of a wealthy judge in Charleston graces one end of the room, and an Atlanta dowager lends an air of gentrification to the other. I asked him when he's going to get around to painting that captivating wife of his, and he said as soon as he's rich enough to paint for love again. I said I'd be too bent and wrinkled to have my portrait done by that time, and he said—well, I'll spare you what he said because it was a poetic misquotation of Marlowe that would make your head hurt. Anyway, I'm certainly not complaining; he's happy with his setup, and though I know he'll be keeping the road hot between Atlanta and Charleston delivering paintings and photographing subjects and interviewing potential clients, it's what keeps the lights on these days (and Queenie in premium dog food). I think a little country retirement will be good for his art in the long run. And I promise to remove the drop cloth from the dining room table when you visit so that we can entertain you in proper style.

I really can't wait for you to see it, Sarah: high-ceilinged and airy, with tall windows in every room that you can raise right up and step out onto the porch. There's an absolute embarrassment of fireplaces, opulent with white marble and crystal girandoles (which Sam has forbidden me to touch and of which I'm righteously terrified), and the cornices are raptures of acanthus leaves and fruit and flowers. It's so well preserved it feels almost uncanny at times. My writer's imagination has peopled it with a cast of charming characters: courtly gentlemen with tongues of angels and hearts of lions; delicate ladies in acres of silk, so cinched and corseted they look as though they might break in the middle; fretful little grannies in lace caps who ring for their breakfast with silver bells, and the lithe, dark-skinned girls who scurry to answer, their gentle ministrations belying the bird-like fury for freedom beating behind the calm eyes. I've even thrown in a faithful hound or two for Queenie's sake, and a few Arabians out in the stable.

In spite of all native skepticism, the first time we looked at the house I couldn't help asking the leasing agent, Mrs. Wilbur, if it happened to be haunted, and she stared at me as if I had just inquired whether her grandfather had two heads. I could see exactly what she was thinking: *Oh no, one of those crackpot writer-types seeking scandal under every bush.* But unfortunately, she hastened to assure me that the Farnhams are far too respectable a family for any such nonsense as ghosts and hauntings. (It's a great-niece of old Elizabeth Farnham who owns the place now, and she was the great-great-great granddaughter of the man who built it, so you can see it's quite the family affair.) If I get too desperate with my own story I might resort to digging for skeletons amid the archives of the peerless Farnhams, but I certainly would not have admitted that to the agent. She seemed dismayed enough by my impiety as it was. There was a distinct chill in her bearing for the rest of the interview. She was kind enough to mention on leaving, however, that if we took the place, we'd best keep the gate locked at the end of the drive as much as possible.

"Vagrants," she elucidated. "They cut across the fields here to get to the highway from South N—. It's *unincorporated*," she added, as if that explained everything.

"But if they come on foot," I persisted, "what good are gates and locks? Couldn't they just hop over?"

Mrs. Wilbur eyed me with exquisite forbearance. "Old Mrs. Farnham kept a dog," she replied, with a doubtful glance at Queenie. Regrettably, Mrs. Wilbur had witnessed Queenie's initial trouble with the stairs, and I'm afraid our girl has disgraced herself irrevocably. At least in Mrs. Wilbur's book which, I'm inclined to think, is long on accounts and short on humor.

Well, I imagine I should sign off now. I fear the length of this first letter may set a precedent I'll find impossible to sustain.

—Robin

October 6, 20—

Dear Sarah,

This week has been so uneventful I have reason to fear for toad-sonnets in my future. It has been raining for six days straight and I think it's so demoralized my imagination I can't even make up entertaining tidbits for your reading pleasure.

Let me see. Sam forgot to add the water to the percolator one morning, the upshot being we were obliged to buy another percolator. Why is something so inconvenient so expensive? But Sam swears by percolated coffee. He says—

Oh dear, I am boring myself, so I can only imagine what I'm putting you through.

Let me try again: I've been having the oddest recurring dream since we moved in: so bland and repetitive it's exasperating. Every night I hear a faint, hollow plunk, followed by a scattering sound, like rice being thrown out on a wood floor. What follows is a low moan, which I wake to find was merely Sam snoring. Yes, that's it. And, yes, I realize that there are few things on earth more eye-glazingly tedious than an account of other peoples' dreams. Lawful heart, have I stooped to that?

Okay, here's something: I saw one of Mrs. Wilbur's vagrants the other day, a woman. She was crossing the eastern pasture, up along a dark row of pines at the fence line, and being the impulsive creature that I am, I jumped up from my desk and raced out to see if she needed anything. I was halfway across the field before I caught her attention, and I must either have offended her or frightened her senseless, as she stopped and stared without a word. I know I can be a bit short on tact when a humanitarian fit seizes me, but her expression reigned me in somewhat, devoid as it was of all warmth and interest. She looked *hollow*, poor soul, like a soldier trudging back into a losing battle, and I immediately felt the imposition of my presence. Sorrow is such a private thing, you know, particularly the sorrow of a stranger. One just doesn't meddle with a despair like that. So I held back at a respectful distance while she turned and resumed her weary course over the brittle, sundried grass. She didn't *look* poverty-stricken, but then again, her clothes were totally out of season: a plain, pale shirt-waist dress with no sleeves (I wore a sweater, as a chill has crept into these early autumn afternoons) and a pair of well-worn ballet flats—not exactly proper gear for cutting cross country. At any rate, I want to remember her eyes so that I can give them to a character in my book. Not to seem merce-nary, but they were so lovely and so sad, like dark wells of serenity.)

I'm too dispirited to write more until the sun comes out again. In my next letter I shall describe in flowering terms both the interior and the aspect of my darling writing room up under the eaves. However, as I have already claimed far more of your time than I have any right to, and as I fear an utter dearth of newsworthy items for future correspondence, I will refrain.

—Robin

ROBIN ELIOT BLAKELY
CANDLEWOOD
C—, SOUTH CAROLINA

October 13, 20—

Dear Sarah,

I am seated at my desk today in such good faith that if you looked closely you could just make out the halo glinting about my head. For four days running I have planted my person in this unforgiving chair and resolutely pounded out page upon page of unmitigated rubbish. I told Sam that I can't even print it out to look over properly as the waste of paper would contribute to world's deforestation, and I won't have that on my conscience along with everything else. Drivel notwithstanding, my fingers have been moving virtuously over the keyboard (I keep checking for calluses) for two hours at a stretch, twice a day. I may delete every word when evening falls, but at least I am remembering how to type. (And at the very least I could hire myself out as a stenographer—if only I knew shorthand.)

At any rate, it's a relief to clear my desk of modern devices and allow my thoughts to stretch and spread over this creamy expanse of paper. What do you think of my new letterhead? Isn't it gorgeous? Sam surprised me with a stout box of stationery he'd ordered after I had expressed my intention to write you, and I was so moved I broke down and cried. Really, I did—even Sam was taken aback. But there was just something about seeing my name engraved above the house's name that seemed to settle all the ruffled feathers of my soul—like stumbling into the warmth of home when I didn't even realize I had been lost. This luxurious ream of watermarked paper means I really belong here, you know, if only for a year.

(Oh, Sarah, suddenly I can't bear to think past this year.)

But I'm here now, and I've never felt so fully present in my life. Every morning I wake up early and wander over the property with Queenie. There are two pastures: the small one you drive through approaching the house, and a larger one to the east that I particularly love. At dawn it looks like a celestial sea, all aglint with golden light and heaving under a burden of misty shadows. I know it's only ordinary broom sedge kindled by an ordinary sun, but it's so miraculous I can hardly bear to miss it—and this from the woman who must needs be dragged from her bed in the city by an extraordinary series of alarms and propped up with the blessed black stimulant the moment her feet hit the floor. I get up now without aid of either clock or coffee pot, joining Sam for his second cup and my first on the back porch after my morning's ramble. It rained one morning last week—the first since I've discovered the celestial sea—and I was so disappointed I could have thrown a temper tantrum. (Instead I took it out on my heroine, venting my vexation in a smallpox epidemic that left her so pock-marked as to be entirely unrecognizable. Don't feel too sorry for her—the whole affair was committed to the round file before the keyboard had cooled. But it did make me feel better.)

There's just something otherworldly about that particular pasture at that particular time of day: it just feels, I don't know, kind of *thin*. Like things could *get through*, if that makes any sense. The only other place I've ever experienced a comparable temptation to contemplate transparency between the dimensions (if there is such a thing) was that ruined monastery we came across in the Black Mountains of Wales—do you remember? We were such kids, tramping over those brooding red hills with our overstuffed backpacks and our overstuffed brains, far too sophisticated to let beauty awe us overmuch. But that place made us silent. We came upon it in a mist, as I recall; the hollow cloisters enveloped us before we hardly knew where we were, and under a sort of benevolent enchantment we sat on a moss-grown pile of debris and just listened—for perhaps the first time in our lives. Then we drank from that crystal-cold stream nearby. And when we got up from our knees, for all the world as if we'd been praying, you spoke the only words either of us uttered in that place. You said, "As cold waters to a thirsty soul, so is good news from a far country."

I stared at you, not because the words seemed ill-fitting, but because they echoed a deep refrain I'd heard in my own head. I didn't really know my Bible (know it even less now, I regret to say), but I've always thought that verse one of the most electrifying in the English language, hinting at things one always hoped were true but couldn't bear to believe. Of course it's all sentimental nonsense, leftover ideals from a less-complicated age (or, worse yet, pure, prosaic Solomonian practicality). But it made me *warm*, somehow, to hear you say it. Like the memory of a fairytale one loved as a child, or a friendly hand in the dark.

We never talked about it later, but I came as close to faith that day as I imagine I ever will in this life. The magic of unseen things was so thick and strong in that place it made me want to believe—in something, *anything*. Who knows, perhaps it was just an accident of altitude changes and the chocolate bar I'd eaten for breakfast, but I couldn't quite escape the conviction that something yet lived amid those ruined aisles that was invisible to the naked eye. Not something unwholesome necessarily, but a force so indomitable, so *undying*, even centuries of silence and decay could not wholly extricate it. I hadn't the faintest idea what such a force might be, and if I've thought of the incident since, it's been merely to wonder that anything could make me teeter with such peril on the precipice of credulity. Imaginative writer I may be, friend Sarah, but you know as well as I do, I'm a rationalist to the back collar button of my soul. I *want* to believe in ghosts and fairies and mangers in Bethlehem. But the powers that be have given me a perfectly reasonable mind that just won't allow it. Sadly, there is an explanation for everything in this benighted era of ours; the Golden Age is over, and "Pan is dead—Great Pan is dead."

In spite of reason, however, (or, perhaps, specifically because of it), I've been haunted all these years by that memory of Wales, recalling it occasionally, in much the way a man long sober might remember the warmth and sting of a good whisky and soda. But it wasn't until I came here that I realized I've been seeking a repeat of it—not until that first morning in the pasture, when I saw the sunrise crack the edge of the world with a rupture of saffron and fire, summoning wraiths from the earth and routing that dark rank of eastern pines in a golden van, that I knew I was in any real danger. (Sentiment, you know, and all the wishful thinking that comes with it, is an addiction we moderns can ill-afford: the only real safely in this brutal world of ours lies in material things we can see and name and comprehend.) Nevertheless, the sense of inhabiting space with an unseen energy seized me once more as it's not done since that silent space of frozen time we passed together at the monastery, and it sent a tremor through me, not only for the sake of my own reason, but for Reason itself. My head insists it is all a very scientific combination of mist and moisture, warmth and light—but, somehow, my heart won't have it. I find myself drawn daily to that place as inexorably as Sherlock Holmes to his opium dens, and if the exaltation is not quite as potent as I remember, then I am all the more keen to pursue it the next day.

It's not only the pasture at dawn that tempts me to "suspend disbe-lief," as Coleridge would say, though the longing for—almost the memory of—impossible things lingers there most poignantly. It's the sunset light filling the front hall with a radiance that makes the chandelier crystals paint quivering rainbows on the wainscoting and walls, and the way those tall windows throw back the firelight and candlelight like stars burning in the black mirror of a midnight sea. And, perhaps, dearest of all, the lovely little muslin-framed watercolor that is the view from the window of my writing room: I've asked Sam to paint it for me in earnest, for even Keats would grudge me this magic casement of mine. It looks out on the inimi-table eastern pasture, with a flash of silver river beyond the tree line and a glimpse of the peach orchard near at hand. Of course, there are no peaches this time of year, but I can only imagine the splendor of blossom and bee-life in spring, and the ambrosial sweetness of its summer burden. (Sam says the peaches won't have much of a chance, given the number of squirrels abroad, but Queenie took that as a deliberate insult. You should have seen the furrow of that brow of hers: it was downright insolent.)

Such splendors abroad are an agreeable contrast to the homely charms within: the ceiling is low and slanted at precocious angles, painted a soothing shade of palest blue—just the color of a summer sky washed with clouds. My desk is tucked under the gable before the magic casement, and the room closes in companionably behind me with a jumble of mismatched furniture and bric-a-brac too homely to be admitted in any other part of the house. There is a white-painted curio cabinet with bowed front and glass doors that's missing a foot, a wicker rocking chair deceptively cushioned in faded chintz that tries to swallow you whole if you're silly enough to sit in it, and a washstand with a cracked jug and no bowl at all. The walls are papered in bluebells, unapologetically sweet, and, if you'll believe it, there's even a handmade hooked rug on the floor.

To the left of the desk (a battered Eastlake monstrosity that looks like it's been tossed around on the bottom of the ocean), there's the wraith of a small oval picture staining the wallpaper. I've searched every nook and cranny for the picture itself, but to no avail. My curiosity has been piqued, however—why that one missing, when the walls are bespattered with dozens of others? There are yellowed prints from an art book affixed with thumbtacks—mostly Corots and Delacroixs—and generic landscapes, and even a perfunctory sampler or two. But no photographs, and nothing to correspond to that taunting oval shape in the alcove. It surprises me, really—the family seems to have been scrupulous about removing all identifiable personal effects from the rest of the house (crystal girandoles and needlepoint footstools there might be in abundance, but not so much as a grocery receipt in a drawer), but here it looks as though nothing has been touched. Nothing, of course, but that tantalizing picture. The curio is stuffed with trinkets both fine and inferior, there are seashells and bird feathers on the windowsill, and when we first came, there was even a little glass bottle of dried-out ferns on the desk. (It felt like a desecration to throw them out.) It's as if a previous occupant had merely stepped out for a stroll—absconding irrationally with that sole picture—but that's impossible: Mrs. Wilbur told me that the house had been vacant for over a year, ever since old Elizabeth Farnham went into a nursing home. It just doesn't make sense. The mystery of the thing is driving me mad.

Speaking of mad, I'm still having that annoying dream. I wonder if there's something psychoanalytical about a writer dreaming of rice (or what sounds like it) scattering over a bare floor. A fertile imagination, *peut-être*?

Sam just popped his head around the door to tell me that a package had arrived with your name as sender. You dear—I would say something conventional like "you shouldn't have," but you'd know I was lying. Birthdays remain among the high holy days in my book, and even though mine's not till Thursday, I'm already entering that period of indulgence and excess typical of the festivity with which I observe the phenomenon of yet another journey around that bright star we call the Sun.

I might just open it with a glass of champagne.

Yours,

Robin

ROBIN ELIOT BLAKELY
CANDLEWOOD
C—, SOUTH CAROLINA

October 16, 20—

Sarah,

Just a quick note to thank you for the exquisite gift. I've never so much as *seen* a glass pen, much less had the fortune to write with one. *Un*fortunately, you can evaluate my prowess based on the amount of ink blots and splotches with which this missive is adorned, but I swear, had you been privy to earlier attempts, you would be duly impressed by my progress. The ink is lovely, too, the very color of violets, and perfumed so delicately as to suggest the essence of violets themselves.

Speaking of perfume, the funniest thing happened yesterday—my actual birthday, you know. I was sitting up here in my eyrie, practicing flourishes with my glass pen (of course), when suddenly I was so assailed with the scent of freesias I looked around, thinking Sam had placed some in the room as a surprise. There were none, but seeing as he knows they're a favorite of mine, and seeing as Sam can't carry off a surprise in a croker sack, I went in search of them. I looked in the bedroom, the kitchen, and the front parlor, but still no freesias. I found Sam, however, in the dining room, paintbrush in one hand and gin and tonic in the other, regarding the Dowager with a surly eye.

"So, where are they?" I inquired, arch as an Austen heroine.

"Where are what?" he answered absently, without taking his eyes from the canvas.

"The freesias," I insisted. "The ones you got me for my birthday."

He looked at me then.

"Oh, Birdie, I'm sorry," he said. "I didn't get you any—I looked at the Food Mart when I went into town, but it seems they don't have them," he cleared his throat, "this time of year."

I was thoroughly flummoxed. "But—I *smelled* them," I insisted, somewhat petulantly. "I'm absolutely certain."

He set down his paintbrush and stepped across the room to kiss me on the top of my head.

"Wishful thinking, Birdlet," he said. "Next year you'll have bushel baskets of freesias—I promise. As long as I get this portrait done."

It's the oddest thing, though. I know I smelled them, Sarah. The scent is unmistakable—and my nose is unfaultable where freesias are concerned.

Warmly,

Robin

ROBIN ELIOT BLAKELY
CANDLEWOOD
C—, SOUTH CAROLINA

October 20, 20—

Gifted One,

I read your essay in the *Lyrae*, and if I didn't love you so much, I'd hate you. Brilliant work, Sarah. I especially loved the way you drew out the uses of poetry, not merely as an expression of human emotion but as a conduit of subconscious wisdom. Indeed, as you put it, "we are more than we know." Or, at least, *you* are. If you're not named editor-in-chief within the year, I shall follow Mrs. Jennings' inimitable lead and eat my bonnet.

Nothing so auspicious in these quarters. Queenie caught a mole in the garden Tuesday and it went to her head so completely she's been impossible to live with since. She's such a little transplant—you'd think she'd never seen a sidewalk, much less a dog park. Believe me, when a city-bred terrier-mix starts putting on countrified airs, one can hardly squeeze oneself into the same room with her ego.

Sam finished The Dowager and he goes to Atlanta Monday to deliver her. I asked him why he didn't paint the whiskers on her chin—I saw them myself the day he photographed her—and he threw a (clean) paintbrush at me. Promise me, Sarah, if I ever get that old and that rich, you'll tell me if I have whiskers on my chin. I know I can't rely on Sam; men are useless in such matters.

In other news, I have successfully managed to outsmart my better self and avoid my desk these six days running with an almost supernatural campaign of distraction. I have pottered and hacked in the ruined garden; I have taken Queenie on so many walks she all but slinks around a corner when she sees me coming; I have dragged Sam down into my debauchery by producing innumerable pots of tea at all hours of the day, wheedling him to "take a break" with me.

"How do you take a break from not doing anything?" he asked yesterday afternoon, when I brought in the second tea tray of the day at five minutes past three.

I won't pretend (at least to you) that I don't know exactly what he's talking about. Work is the only reasonable "break" from this pathetic indolence of mine. But here's the thing, Sarah, the sticking point I just can't seem to pry myself past: I'm afraid.

I know what you're thinking: *Of course you, are, you ninny. We all are. Now get back to work.*

But Sarah—and this is a secret I can't even bring myself to tell Sam—it's not the work I'm afraid of, nor the idea of sitting in all that wordless silence. I'm not even afraid of failure anymore, I don't think; all these tortured months have driven that to the back of my mind where the least of concerns lie gathering dust. No, it's none of that. Sarah—good grief, this sounds ridiculous—*but it's my writing room I'm afraid of.*

There. I said it. Rest assured I am laughing at myself as heartily as you are laughing at me. (I can all but see the wry twist of your mouth, summoning that cynical dimple with which the gods graced your otherwise unflappable composure.) But let me explain, if I can. At the very least, the attempt to put it down in words might discharge some of the shock of the thing, and cast events in a more benign light. And at best? Well, I'm writing *something*, which is more than can be said for the past week together.

Last Wednesday was humid and dour, and I had a mood to match it. I went out walking early, but there was no sunrise under all those clouds to bewitch me into better spirits, and when I got back to the house, Sam had drunk all the coffee, which made me cross as a cat with a knot in its tail. I betook myself to my writing room—*after* making a fresh pot of coffee—and opened the door with a sense of sweet release. Here were no injustices—climatic or domestic—to rankle the soul, only blessed quiet and solitude, the twin necessities of a writer's life.

As soon as I came into the room, however, something felt—*off.* I don't know if I've quite articulated the connection I have with this little nest of mine up under the eaves; there's something almost womblike about the comfort and belonging I've known there from the very start. I claimed it without hesitation the first day we came—but it had already claimed me. Suddenly, however, standing there in the doorway with my coffee tray and my notebook, it wasn't mine anymore. An almost nauseating feeling of intrusion took my breath, like going into the wrong hotel room or taking someone's seat at the symphony (both of which I've done, so I ought to know). I stood there in an awful hesitation, glancing tentatively around, when it began to dawn on me that it was colder within the room than it was out in the hallway. The windows were fogged up and there was a distinct chill that pricked up the hair on my arms and crinkled along the back of my neck.

I stepped back inadvertently, as though the cold were a physical occupant I had disturbed. It was then I saw something that nearly made me drop my tray. I stumbled to the desk and set it down with a bang, staring hard at the magic casement. Good God, Sarah, I'd give anything if I could unsee it—but there, traced upon the glass with what looked like nothing less than a human finger was a suggestion of letters, backwards, as though printed on the outside: "oem" was all I could make out, but there were fragments on either side. I shudder even to write it—it summons the horror of those characters, , from which the condensation had just started to run.

Once the first paralysis of fear had subsided, I did what any rational woman would do: I screamed for my husband. Sam came running (with a solicitude that immediately exonerated him from the affair of the coffee), still clutching a turpentine-soaked rag in his hand. Seeing I was in evident possession of both wits and appendages, he cast his eyes inquiringly about the room. Steadying my hand, I pointed at the window. He stepped over and inspected it closely.

"Hmm," was his authoritative assessment.

"Is that all you can say?" I demanded. "There's a *word* on the window, Sam."

"I wouldn't call it a word."

"Well, at least you see it too," I said with more peevishness than I intended.

"What do you mean? Of course I see it. Is this what made you scream?"

The combined nonchalance and amusement in his tone made me want to scream again, for a different reason. I didn't, you'll be glad to hear—I folded my arms and tilted my chin.

"Yes. It scared me. Do you think it's some kind of a joke?"

"Well, if it is, there's not much to it." He shrugged his shoulders. "Probably just left over from a previous tenant. I'll bet the windows up here haven't been washed since 1964."

"I washed them myself," I insisted, "the week we moved in. Besides, the writing's on the outside."

"All the more reason to think it predates us. A fluke, yes, but a reasonable one, Birdie."

I was far from convinced. The icy sting on the back of my neck pricked up again. Who in their right mind would risk life and limb on those mossy cedar shakes just to finger a few letters on the outside of a window? It didn't make sense.

Sam smiled and squeezed my arm.

"Listen, lady, I've got a date downstairs with the judge's daughter," he said. "She's due next weekend, you know, so let's keep the fire alarms to a minimum."

He turned to go, but I called after him. "Sam—what would make the windows fog up—on the outside of the room, I mean?"

He paused in the doorway, considering.

"I imagine it would have to be cooler indoors than out. I'm a painter, though—not a scientist."

"Sam," I said again, and he turned once more, though his smile was slightly haggard. "Sam—are the windows fogged up—in the rest of the house?"

His brow contracted for a second. "No, come to think of it. They're not."
We stared at one another in silence until Sam broke the spell. "It's a fluke, I'm telling you, honey. If you can't put up with a few oddities, you'll never make it in an old house. There's a reason for everything—though everything isn't always plainly reasonable. Just lean into it, Robin, sit with the mystery a bit. And then, for heaven's sake, write your book." He leaned over and popped me with his painter's rag. "*Derriere* in chair."

I heard his retreating footsteps on the stairs, and the heavy click of the dining room door as he shut himself back in with his work. Then I turned to look at the magic casement again. Already the moisture had gathered in little rivulets that were chasing each other down the glass so that the letters were nearly obliterated. I went to the desk and pulled out the chair with every good intention, but I could not make myself sit down. The place felt so—*full*—and I so unwanted within it. Blushing with shame (I blush now to confess it) I picked up my tray and went out, closing the door behind me.

That I, a strong-minded female of the twenty-first century, should be thus dismissed in my own home—it's appalling. Not to mention embarrassing. I don't know what to make of it, Sarah; my native good sense is properly horrified at such frailty—but, somehow, I haven't quite been able to look common sense in the eye since last Monday. Maybe I'm growing morbid, being so much alone, or maybe the rural life doesn't agree with me as much as I thought it did. But I just can't shake the chill of that writing on the windowpane—for writing I'm convinced it was. It seems to have soured things for me, which is unfortunate. I love this place as much as I ever did—though I love my own sanity more.

I wish you could visit before November. I need the sound of your laughter in my ears to scatter this absurdity. Do think about it.

Yours,

—R

ROBIN ELIOT BLAKELY
CANDLEWOOD
C—, SOUTH CAROLINA

October 27, 20—

Dear Sarah,

Sam left for Atlanta yesterday. He asked me—rather pointedly, I'm afraid—if I didn't want to come with him, but I declined (with much more flippancy than I felt). Between us, I wish I *had* gone with him; my nerves are nearly shredded after one night alone, and after what happened today, the thought of another threatens to send me over the edge. But it's just for that reason I stayed: I won't let this thing beat me. I won't be at the mercy of anything so irrational as fear. Fear is what I've felt this week, though I've resisted it at every turn. The embarrassment of that last letter must have steeled me—that, and the knowledge that I'll have to account for my time in this one. But each day I've marched into that room under the eaves (I can't quite bring myself to call it 'mine' again) and thumped my coffee down on the desk. I've written reams of twaddle and consumed way more caffeine than is good for me and worked myself into the beginnings of a pinched nerve in my neck.

And yet, the fear remains, crouching low when I'm most wary of it, only to spring at my throat when I dare to suppose I've routed it at last. Last night was interminable. The dark seemed to usher in a host of shadows I'd never noticed before, whispering along the walls and gathering in corners and under the stairs with a horrible hostility. I know it's all in my head—this imagination of mine has two faces, as do all good servants of the Muse—but it can be very difficult to remember that when there's no Sam here to keep me from taking myself too seriously. I regret to say that

I conceded to both fear and imagination in the matter of sleeping arrangements: when darkness fell I simply could not force myself to mount those stairs (stairs, mind, with which Queenie has had occasion to remind me she wants no part). I needed the warmth of a living body beside me to hold that hungry dark at bay, and since Queenie was the only candidate, I invited her to sleep with me on the sofa in Sam's studio. Queenie, ecstatic to resume a habit which only the weeks we've spent in this house has interrupted, bounded up beside me and commenced to snore with an enviable alacrity. (That dog either has nothing on her conscience or she tipples the gin when I'm not looking—I swear she could sleep through an air raid.)

A long, eerie night ensued in which a thousand horrors occurred to my wakeful mind and absolutely nothing happened—or at least nothing that I couldn't account for as ordinary noises of the house, to which I've already grown accustomed: a bump and rattle on the roof was a walnut falling from a tree and rolling down over the shakes; a low grating sound was the furnace clicking on in the basement; a ghastly, maniacal chuckle was the screech owl in the woods we've heard every night since we came. Nevertheless, I didn't sleep a wink, and nearly wept with relief when the first grey promise of dawn began to creep over the world. I was so exhausted I didn't even feel like taking my morning ramble—though, judging by the clearness of that growing light and the one pure, cold note of greeting from a white throated sparrow in the cedar tree outside, it promised to be a fine one. Instead I rolled over on the sofa, to Queenie's disgruntlement, and slept for two hours.

I felt better when I got up, and even more so after a shower and a cup of coffee. The autumn sunlight streamed in through the uncurtained windows, making the house friendly again, and I felt so warmed by it that I threw open the front and back doors in welcome. By mutual consent, Queenie and I established ourselves catlike in a sunny patch on the front steps, I with my laptop and she with her bone, and while she gnawed herself into a state of euphoric transcendence, I proceeded to fall into a daydream about my novel. It was the first time that's happened in over a year, so

I imagine I was experiencing a sort of transcendence of my own—after all, you and I both know that reverie is first cousin to actual writing. It was grand: all silken skirts and courtly manners—inspired, no doubt, by my period-appropriate domicile—and so thoroughly was I lost in my own head, that I didn't notice Queenie had left until I glanced down and saw her bone lying on the sun-warmed boards beside me.

It isn't like her to abandon a trophy without burying it first, so I got up to investigate. Just as I stepped down into the yard, however, I caught the low, ominous rumble of her growl coming from inside the front hall. I'm not sure what I expected to find, but what I saw upon entering was my brave little dog, body all a-tremble, standing at the foot of the stairs, looking up. A snarl twitched at the corners of her mouth and that feather-plume tail of hers was curled up over her back in a rigid question mark. Most amazing of all, her front feet were placed on the bottom stair, and she was rocking back and forth as though steeling herself to proceed. Seeing me, she barked, and added a reckless step or two to her conquered ground, but then she froze again with a pathetic whimper.

"Queenie," I said low, almost a whisper, but she didn't heed me. The hackles rose on the back of her neck and she growled again. I must confess, I was feeling uneasy at this point, but I walked to the foot of the stairs, placed my hand resolutely on the newel post, and peered up into the gloom above. There was nothing there.

"Squirrel in the attic, girl?" I murmured, despising the tremble in my voice.

It was insupportable, of course, to feel such groundless dread in the clear light of day. Possibly a bird had gotten in through those open doors—Sam was always warning me about that—or a stray draft had made a noise Queenie didn't like. Just as such cold comfort was taking shape in my mind, however, a familiar sound nearly stopped my heart. It was the door to the gable room: it had creaked open, not with a breeze-borne rush, but as though under the pressure of a steady hand. I heard the light rattle of the knob and a creak of well-known hinges—and then, most horrifying of all, the ominous click of the latch against the plate as the door was pulled to once more.

There was nothing for it, Sarah—I had either to investigate or to tuck Queenie under my arm and run screaming from the house. Fear acted as a potent drug in this case, and though my body felt like it had turned to ice and my heart was pounding out of my chest, I grabbed the banister railing and proceeded up those stairs. Queenie slunk after me, though I told her to stay, but her ears were held back against her head and her proud little tail drooped pitiably. I was glad enough of her quivering company when I reached the door to the gable room, though. My hand hovered over the knob as if it were a hot coal, and I think that both of us were holding our breath.

Before I had a chance to change my mind, I flung open the door and stepped into the room. The scent of freesias was so potent I nearly choked; but for that, the room was undisturbed. A light breeze lifted the curtains at the window I'd left open, fluttering some papers on the desk, and a jay chattered on the roof outside. All of these things seemed so keen to me, so clear and so terribly important: the sound, the movement, the scent. But the room was empty; nothing human or otherwise, save Queenie, who was still shivering on the threshold beside me..

I say it was empty—but Sarah, somehow that isn't quite true. I don't know if I can make you understand the energy that was in that place, as though the air were charged with an unseen brightness, but I felt if I closed my eyes for long it would blind me. The voltage—if that's what you can call it, I know of no precedent from which to garner descriptive phrases of such things—was so vibrant it almost crowded me out of the room. A sort-of frantic vitality pervaded, like a bird beating itself senseless against a windowpane and circling round to go at it again. And here's the thing, the incomprehensible, improbable, implausible thing: that energy had an essence which was suddenly invoked in me: not fear, as might be supposed, or misery, or even dread—but *longing*.

Don't ask me how I know this—I couldn't explain it to you if you did. All I know is that Queenie and I stood there together watching something inhabit that room that we could not see. Well, at least I couldn't. But after a moment or two of enraptured silence, Queenie inched past me and sat down in her most ladylike pose, tail swishing gently over the floor. She must have seen something that soothed her, or, at the very least, conquered some inner demon, for she's no longer afraid to come upstairs. She spent the rest of the morning exploring the second floor rooms as if she's discovered a whole new house.

I, on the other hand, came downstairs and had a glass of sherry. I was so shaken I could hardly sit still. I don't know what to make of it, Sarah. I'm sure you've quite given up on me at this point, and are ready to swoop down with stories of imaginative folks who spent too much time alone and went completely off their rockers. Perhaps you're right; perhaps I'm just the kind of person to turn funny in solitude.

Or maybe—just maybe—I'm the kind of person that challenges every assumption but my own. Do I think my house is haunted? It seems too small a question, somehow. I've always both doubted and wished there was a world beyond my ken, but easily refuted it. The great point that keeps rising to the surface of my mind is this: if there is such a world, what might it cost me to glimpse it—and turn away my eyes as if I had not seen?

—R

To: Sarah Willcox   Sent: 10/29/20—2:59 PM
SUBJECT: fool's errand

Sarah,

Yes, I've conceded to the present day in the matter of communication, but
only this once, as I'm in Charleston with Sam and the judge's daughter for
the weekend (he says her name is Chelsea, by the way) and as I'm in a great
hurry to enlighten you on my latest scheme. Sam said he thought it would
be good for me to go with him on this delivery, get me out of the house, you
know, and I pretended to believe he meant it for my entertainment and not
my mental balance. I know he's worried after what happened when he was in
Atlanta last week, (and, judging from the note you dashed off on receipt of
my last letter, I gather that you are as well), but I can't help thinking the best
way to clear up any odd sensations and experiences I've had at Candlewood
is to prod the mystery a bit. Lean into it, as Sam has said.

So that's exactly what I'm going to do. When Sam said Charleston, I
immediately remembered the leasing agent had mentioned that Elizabeth
Farnham's niece lives just outside of the city, on the Charles River. I called
her saying I wanted to do some research on the house (I do), and though
a bit cagey, she agreed to see me. I'm going out to her place this afternoon
while Sam is delivering Chelsea, and I don't mean to return without some
answers (or, at least a little gossip).

At this distance, the mystery is enticing. Was there an inconsolable war
widow of the Great Conflict, or a remorseful son who returned too late
to bid a dying mother farewell? My imagination is running rampant, and
while it's easier to be playful about the matter when I'm away from the
house, I promise you, I won't so much as breathe the word "ghost." Not
even once. It might give Miss Farnham the vapors.

—R

ROBIN ELIOT BLAKELY
CANDLEWOOD
C—, SOUTH CAROLINA

November 3, 20—

Dearest,

I don't know quite how to say this, but it seems the affair is at an end. The events of the past week have culminated in a climax both unmistakable and, to my mind, final, but in order for you to fully appreciate it, I must first enlighten you on my interview with Edith Farnham. That was the beginning of all this ending, you might say—unless of course it was already well underway and I only happened to step in at the crucial moment. You know how prone I am to flatter my own indispensability—but, Sarah, I can't escape the conviction that somehow I was *supposed* to be a part of this.

Edith welcomed me with a friendly, albeit restrained, formality. She's an exquisite specimen of the Southern dame: silver hair cut in a wedge, honeyed accent, ring-encrusted fingers. We had tea on her terrace overlooking the lawn, all Limoges and family silver, and it was going quite civilly until I happened to mention that there had been a couple of "disturbances" at Candlewood in the weeks since we'd moved in. She set down her cup and looked at me piercingly.

"Disturbances?" she repeated, with an offhand air that but thinly veiled her evident interest.

At the expense of my dignity, I told her everything—the scents, the sounds, the dreams I was having. I even tried to elucidate the experience Queenie and I had in the gable room last week, but she stopped me before I had half begun.

"Yes, yes, yes," she suddenly sighed, with a wave of her jeweled hand. "Yes, my dear. I know. She did so love freesias."

It was my turn to stare. There was an air of concession about her as she leaned back into the cushions of her chair and interlaced her fingers meditatively.

"I suppose I shall have to enlighten you. Not that I would have placed a tenant of mine in danger for all the world." She leaned forward suddenly and patted my knee with a matronly gesture. "I assure you, Noémi wouldn't hurt a soul, in life or in death. I *had* hoped it was just me. It's comforting somehow to know I'm not the only one to believe that Candlewood is haunted— but it's very inconvenient."

I nearly choked on my tea.

"So—nothing I've said is a surprise to you?"

Edith shook her head gravely. "I meant no deceit," she insisted.

"But you left her room undisturbed."

"I did," Edith assented, "Except—,"

"Except for the picture of her by the desk—you were afraid I might recognize her."

"You are very perceptive for a young woman," she replied, with the slightest ghost of a smile. But I noticed that her eyes had grown suddenly bright with unshed tears.

"I'm a writer." I grinned back at her. "I'm paid to be perceptive. But I would like to see the picture of—of Noémi," my mouth fumbled with the foreign inflection. "Just out of curiosity. I assume you still have it."

"Of course I do," Edith said, rising from her chair with an almost haughty aspect. "My family hasn't thrown anything away in a hundred and seventy years. Besides, I'd never part with a picture of Noémi. She was like a daughter to me."

"Wait," I cried, arresting her as she turned to go into the house. "You— you *knew* her?"

It occurred to me that I had been imagining this intersecting of dimensions (for lack of a better expression) as a faint but romantic aroma of the far-distant past—I'd never dreamed my supposed "companion" was contemporary.

"Yes, I knew her," Edith replied steadily, though her chin wavered. "I was her godmother."

When she brought the picture, I stared at it like it was one of the crown jewels: inside a lovely little walnut oval, there gleamed the radiant smiles of two women, one of which was Edith herself. It had probably been taken a decade ago, or more, for Edith's hair was not quite so silver, and the lines about her mouth were not nearly so pronounced. But it wasn't Edith's face that held my gaze spellbound—it was the other woman, slight and young, with ivory skin and eyes like dark wells of serenity. Eyes that I had seen before.

"Noémi," Edith mused gently. "It means 'pleasant.'" Her gaze grew soft as I handed the picture back again and she looked at it in silence for a moment. "She was nothing but. The gentlest thing you ever saw. She took things too hard, though. If only Noémi was as kind to herself as she was to everyone else."

The story was brief, if tragic, as all too many life stories are: Noémi was the daughter of one of Edith's school friends who married a Frenchman, and when both Edith's friend and her husband were killed in a boating accident, the grief-stricken Noémi paid a visit to her godmother which lasted nearly fifteen years. She lived at Candlewood with the two Miss Farnhams, becoming a companion to the elderly Elizabeth as her health deteriorated. Seeing as Noémi had started a nursing course before leaving France, it seemed a natural bent for her arts, but Edith and Elizabeth occasionally worried that the life was too narrow for a young woman with beauty and promise. Noémi, however, seemed perfectly content to live out her days in quiet obscurity—"Never really got over the death of her parents," Edith confided. "I told you—she took things too hard. She was raised a good Catholic girl, but that Gallic blood was a fire in her veins, for all her outer tranquility."

Being the sole dispenser of all the old woman's medications, Noémi took her charge very seriously, rarely going out in the evenings and scarcely allowing even Edith to administer a dose. It was a complex regimen with potentially hazardous interactions, and Noémi usually sorted pills on a weekly basis to avoid last minute mistakes. For all her loyalty and order, however, the girl had one vice: a tendency to become so engrossed in a book she lost all sense of time and place. Her favorite place to read was on the roof just outside her gable window, if you can believe it. I was a bit incredulous, but Edith explained that it reminded her of a girlhood home in France, wherein tall windows opened out onto a flat space of tile that so gathered the sun's wealth as to be warm well into the night. Reading under the stars, she said, reminded her of happier days; suspended thus between heaven and earth she detached more easily into the world of her dreams. Well, our girl was nothing if not eccentric. But she was steadfast as the day is long, according to Edith. They scarcely needed clocks in the house, Noémi was so methodical.

One evening, however, Noémi entered Elizabeth's room in a fluster: it was an hour past the old woman's dose, and the pills hadn't been measured out. She had been reading on the roof, and Edith could hear her berating herself in the next room as her hands flew among the myriad bottles on the dresser. Suddenly, however, there was the sound of something hitting the floor and the rice-like scattering of tablets over the hardwoods, followed by a moan of such mortal anguish Edith thought it must be Elizabeth. She ran into the room, to find Elizabeth strangely rigid among the pillows, and Noémi, equally motionless, standing by the bed with her hand clamped over her mouth and her eyes wide with horror.

While Edith leaned over the prone figure, trying to determine if she was breathing, she heard Noémi stumble out of the room behind her. "*Dieu, maudis-moi, Dieu, maudis-moi,*" she muttered brokenly. Then the door of the gable room closed behind her with what Edith recalls now as an ominous click. All she could think of in the moment, however, was her aunt Elizabeth—only after the ambulance arrived and the paramedic had confirmed it was a stroke had she time to think of Noémi. And by then, of course it was too late.

They found her on the floor of her room, an empty bottle of Elizabeth's pills on the rug nearby and the crumpled attempt at a note in her convulsed hand.

"She thought she killed her—thought she mixed up a dose," Edith told me. "It was as straightforward a stroke as the doctor had ever seen, and he assured me that not even a boatload of properly timed drugs could have staved it off. My poor, darling, foolish girl! What sin—what unforgivable impetuosity—to take her own life! Yet all I can fault her for is refusing to believe that she was loved. She never could quite accept that, you know, though she herself loved with a passion that was almost fierce at times."

Elizabeth Farham went into a nursing home and lived another six months, while Edith, whose associations were too painful to allow her to stay on alone at Candlewood, moved into town and leased the house. And that was that. Edith, not being a Catholic herself, was unsure what to do in the case of suicide, and, besides, Noémi had not been a regular communicant since she had moved to the States. In the end, Edith decided to say goodbye to Noémi quietly and in her own way. She said it would have been like having her die all over again to see that empty church at a funeral, anyway, as Noémi had so few friends.

"But I scattered her ashes at Candlewood," she told me. "Up along the tree line in the eastern pasture. It was her favorite walk."

Edith and I sipped our tea in silence for a moment or two after she had finished her tale, gazing out over the green lawn in the rare companionability that sometimes occurs between strangers whose thoughts are suddenly consumed with a common interest. Only Edith didn't feel like a stranger anymore—I flatter myself to hope she felt the same way about me. She made me promise to let her know next time I was in Charleston.

"I'm glad there's such a—*sympathetic* person in my house," she said, pressing my hand as I was leaving.

I came back to Candlewood a changed woman, Sarah. You know I'm not in the least degree "religious," but somehow all this imponderabilty suddenly had very little to do with what I've classified as "religion" all my life. I felt possessed by Noémi's story, almost tormented with her grief. I knew her anguish, waking and sleeping, and I knew her desperation to be free of it. She's only been gone a little over a year, but I wonder if it hasn't seemed like centuries to her restless love.

I didn't know what to do—I know so little of anything these days, and for the first time in my life, I'm able to admit it—so I looked up a priest who was willing to perform a funeral rite under such irregular circumstances. I had to go as far afield as Charleston; there weren't many options out here in the sticks, but Fr. Jameson was able to come yesterday and was as fatherly and grave as heart could wish for such an office. The Rite of Committal, he called it, and while he presided, Sam, Queenie and I stood by as mourners. It was very beautiful: the kindly priest in his flowing black vestments, the blessing of the "grave," the simple prayers—over in a matter of moments, but somehow timeless in its significance. Even Queenie seemed awed by the implications of it all.

As we were walking back to the house, Fr. Jameson mentioned how fitting it was to perform such a rite on All Souls. I didn't know what he meant at first, but he explained that it was a day in which believers have historically prayed for those who have died.

"The French lay chrysanthemums on the graves, if I'm not mistaken," he told me with a smile. "But we all remember *des fidèles défunts*. It's one of our essential beliefs, you know: there is a very real bond between the faithful who have gone before and the faithful who remain."

I'm certainly not faithful, but as soon as he had gone, I ran to the flowerbeds skirting the front of the house and pillaged them of every bloom I could lay my hands on. There were a few mums among them, but also some late-blooming zinnias and frothy blue clouds of mist flowers. Arms full, I raced back to the eastern pasture before Sam could ask me what I was up to, but when I got to the tree line I halted in awkward indecision. Then I stooped and resolutely began laying the flowers on the lately consecrated earth, overlapping blossoms in a bright line of color and scent.

Almost without my realizing it, I was uttering words, a soft murmuring that fell in rhythm with my work. "Oh, Noémi, you are loved," I found myself whispering, as close to a prayer as anything that's ever come out of my mouth. "You are loved, loved, *loved*." I haven't the faintest idea where such a conviction came from—all I logically knew of this woman was secondhand. But logic had been unseated for the moment, and something both exquisite and terrifying was pressing into its place, relentless but not forceful, tender, like a gallant cherishing every expectation of admittance.

I came to the last stem and straightened to look back over the flowery wake I had left under the pines. And it was then that I saw her, not twenty feet away. The sun was setting, and the amber light fell full upon her face, touching her head with a nimbus of fire. The chill despair had gone from her aspect, and in its place something ineffable shone: warm and radiant and alive. She seemed clothed with it, and yet it seemed to emanate from her. Her eyes fixed mine with a gaze so penetrating I couldn't have looked away if I wanted to, and a smile tugged at the corners of her mouth. An occultist would say that she was using my energy to take visible form, or some other such tripe. But there was nothing remotely dark about her appearance or my experience of it. On the contrary: her brightness was all gift and grace, warming me like a glass of golden wine.

A bird flew up from a tangle of hedge and honeysuckle under the trees, and she broke her long stare to watch it mount against ramparts of sunstained clouds. In an instant, the smile that had trembled and shimmered flamed out with a brilliance of blinding delight, and she threw back her head, laughing like a child.

Blinking my eyes over sudden tears, I realized she was gone.

I can hardly account for the experiences I've had since I came to this house, or imagine the consequences of admitting them to you, much less to myself. But here is one thing I know to the marrow of my bones, and it changes everything: *there is a far country.*

There is a far country, Sarah, you were right. And the news of it is like cold water to a thirsty soul. I still don't know what it all means. But I finally think I know the name of the force we both encountered at the monastery in Wales: it's Love.

I'm so looking forward to your visit next week. I want to talk about all of these things in person.

I love you, friend,

Robin

Fact: Eric Peters and Thomas McKenzie will survive the zombie apocalypse. David Mitchel will not.

FEAR
by Andrew Peterson

N ow that fear appears
In its right and proper place:
A palpable presence,
Gray and grinning,
But small and weak
And utterly bereft
Of any power
That was not
Given to it.
It insolently lurks
At the moist, mossy edges
Of an otherwise sunny scene.

It looks small and sniveling,
No more able to hurt me
Than a roach in the woodpile,
And I turn from the reek

Of its rot to see the way
The fecund field
Of grass and garden
Turn the wormy wetness
Into a happy feast
For good and growing things.

THIS HAUNTING
by Chris Yokel

D riven by a restlessness,
　　driven on and on
through the cities of men
　　with their glass-metal mountains,
through the bright blazing streets,
　　and their mazes of delight.
Still a voice echoes out
　　around every corner:
　　"We will never be home
　　until the city descends."

Driven on by a longing,
　　driven on and on
through cathedral-columned forests,
　　to the heights of cloud-tossed mountains,
and the valleys swept with shadow
　　where the water falls to streams.
In the flow I hear the echo:
　　"We will not sing the song until
　　the rocks and trees break forth in praise."

Driven on by an emptiness,
    driven on and on
underneath the wheeling stars
    in the vast dark dome of night,
silently alive in the dance of planets.
    In the black between the stars I hear:
    "We will never dance as we ought
    until the loving mover moves us"

Driven on by a turbulence,
    driven on and on
to the storm-tossed oceans,
    foaming and frothing,
moving to moondance
    in the rising and falling.
In the silence between the waves
    it says:
    "We will not rest until the ocean-tamer
    stretches forth his hand."

Driven on by this haunting
    in every corner of creation,
by fragments of a lost song
    we have never heard,
by this understanding when we look
    at light filling up a sky:
Everything is a shadow
    of its future self,
for creation waits
    to fulfill its purpose,
waits to be filled with unshackled glory
    when the ghost, at last, takes on flesh eternal.

THE BLACK HORIZON (PART V)
Story and Illustrations by Jamin Still

THE FALLS

The boat had been falling silently into blackness for days. Jacob stood gripping the rail, watching the stars and planets streak past, watching the Greatest Adventure unfold around him. He waited with expectation, and as he stood, his feet rooted firmly on the deck, the eerie silence was broken. There was a piercing note, vaguely familiar, and a clear birdsong, and the flapping of wings. A shape emerged from the inky blackness and alighted on the rail beside him. The notes faded and the bird spoke.

"Why do you fall, Jacob?"

"Excuse me?"

"Why do you fall? Why... this?"

Jacob was silent for a time as he looked at the bird and traced his journey from the morning of The Hourglass and his father's absence, to the tower, the Sparrows, the Falls, the plunge, and all the blackness and silence since. "This is what I've been working toward my whole life." His hand went instinctively toward his pocket.

The bird cocked its head and gazed at Jacob with its glistening eye. "It will not be enough. This will not be enough. You'll forever be falling and what you hope to find is not at the bottom."

Jacob stared at the bird, its feathers unruffled by the upward-blowing gale, its eye unblinking and steady.

"Come," said the bird. "Fly with me. *This* is the way. *This* is the Greatest Adventure. Only *this* will be enough."

A tightness eased unexpectedly within Jacob. His palms were suddenly moist, his mouth suddenly dry.

"Fly with me," whispered the bird. And then with one last look it spread its wings and ascended into the darkness.

Jacob loosened his grip on the rail. He rubbed one hand across his face. All around him, the wind swirled as the boat plunged down, down, down into the unknown. And somewhere in the darkness far above, the birdsong patiently called to him.

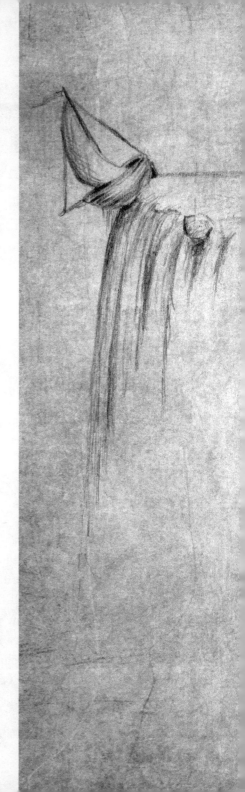

COMMON THINGS
by Chris Yokel

I have never seen
the Grand Canyon with
my own eyes,
but I have seen the pine tree
by the little brook in the woods,
  and that is no small thing.

Fact: Eric Peters saves all his mayonnaise packets for Jonathan Rogers. What Dr. Rogers does with them, no living reptile knows.

by Lewis Graham

I've been very fortunate in this life to work alongside some extraordinarily talented people. At times along the way I have witnessed masters at their crafts. These are people who have found the exact reason they were sent here. I've learned as much as I can from them. My friends have shown me how to make some of the most delicious dishes one could imagine. From embarrassingly rich to breathless restraint, no one held any learning back.

That, family, is not how I eat. It's how I show you love and affection. I eat very simply. I love shady Mexican restaurants and greasy hamburger joints. So this last recipe is one of my favorite meals. As a chef, I have learned to eat cold food quickly. Usually while smoking a cigarette and talking to my beautiful wife for the first time that day.

In the pantry:
1. White bread
2. Doritos (the red ones)

In the fridge:
1. Deli-sliced chicken
2. Mayonnaise

Incredibly complicated directions:
1. Spread mayo on white bread.
2. On one piece, layer the chicken.
3. Stack Doritos on the chicken.
4. Put the lid on it, and with the flat palm of your hand smash it down real good.
5. If your refrigerator has a produce drawer, keep your Mountain Dew in there—it gets icy.
6. Stand in the dark with the refrigerator door open. Eat your sammich. Ignore the fire in your feet and the arthritis in your hands. After all, sometimes your path chooses you.

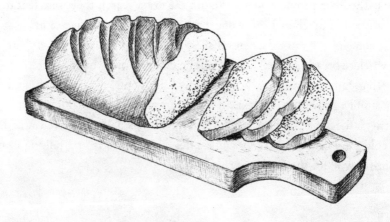

CONTRIBUTORS

SARAH CLARKSON is the author of *Read for the Heart* (a guide to a healthy reading life for families) and *Journeys of Faithfulness* (stories of life and faith for young Christian women). She hails from the dappled foothills of Colorado and plans to write at least one great novel before she dies. In the meantime, she studies literature at Oxford, where she was awarded the 2014 Frederick Buechner Award for creative writing. *(www.ThoroughlyAlive.com)*

LEWIS GRAHAM is one of Nashville's finest chefs, and to prove it he once served us a meal of antelope that was shot from a helicopter with a bow and arrow (the arrow was shot from the helicopter—not the meal of antelope). He's also kept the masses happy for the past two years as Head Chef of the Hutchmoot, a position we hope he'll consent to fill for many years to come.

LANIER IVESTER is a "Southern Lady," in the best and most classical sense, and a gifted writer, in the most articulate and literal sense. She also hand-binds books and lives on a farm with peacocks, bees, sheep, and the governor of Ohio's leg. She and her husband have been known to spend their vacation time in old black-and-white movies. *(www.LaniersBooks.com)*

JONNY JIMISON, also known as "that one guy who draws comics," is one guy who draws comics. *Martin & Marco*, the first volume of his new graphic novel series, is due to hit shelves in January 2015. He lives in Jacksonville, Florida, where he is a freelance illustrator and a builder of Lego spaceships. *(www.JonnyJimison.com)*

DOUGLAS MCKELVEY is the remote descendant of Scottish horse-thieving ancestors, and has already bested the dubious achievements of his predecessors by semi-anonymously penning a handful of books and scripts, writing and directing various video projects, and crafting lyrics to more than 350 songs recorded and released by a variety of artists including Jason Gray, Sanctus Real, and Kenny Rogers.

THOMAS MCKENZIE is the author of *The Anglican Way*, as well as the inimitable host of the One Minute Review and the pastor of Church of the Redeemer in Nashville, Tennessee. Also, he has samurai swords and wears a skull ring. We highly recommend this priest. *(www.OneMinuteReview.com)*

ERIC PETERS is a singer-songwriter who has recorded six solo albums including *Chrome* and *Birds of Relocation*. He's also a painter, a photographer, a curmudgeon, a lawn connoisseur, and a hopeless bibliophile. *(www.EricPeters.net)*

A. S. PETERSON is the author of the Revolutionary War novels *The Fiddler's Gun* and *Fiddler's Green*. He's also the managing editor of Rabbit Room Press and is a nefarious puppeteer who lurks in the shadows, pulling strings, planning Hutchmoots, plotting books, and conspiring to sail away and have bloody adventures.

ANDREW PETERSON is the proprietor of the Rabbit Room and the singer-songwriter of more than ten albums including *After All These Years*, *Light for the Lost Boy*, and *Behold the Lamb of God: The True Tall Tale of the Coming of Christ*. He is also the author of the best-selling, Christy award-winning, *World Magazine* Children's Book of the Year-winning WINGFEATHER SAGA, the final volume of which (*The Warden and the Wolf King*) is currently available whereever great books are sold. *(www.Andrew-Peterson.com)*

RUSS RAMSEY is the author of *Behold the Lamb of God: An Advent Narrative* and *Behold the King of Glory: A Narrative of the Life, Death, and Resurrection of Jesus Christ* (coming in January 2015 from Crossway Books). He is a pastor at Midtown Fellowship in Nashville, Tennessee, and he remains bravely unapologetic in his appreciation of baseball, floating tremolo systems, big hair, Vanderbilt surgeons, and Dutch painters.

Jonathan Rogers is the author of seven books including as the Wilderking Trilogy, *The Charlatan's Boy*, *The World According to Narnia*, and *The Terrible Speed of Mercy*. In the near future he aspires to become the world's foremost authority on the works of Sir Richard Roland, Second Earl of Astley. *(www.Jonathan-Rogers.com)*

Luci Shaw is a charter member of the Chrysostom Society of Writers and is the author of ten volumes of poetry as well as several works of non-fiction including *Breath for the Bones* and *Adventure of Ascent*. She has lectured all over the world on art and spirituality, and the Christian imagination, as well as poetry- and journal-writing as aids to artistic and spiritual growth. She has recently been regaled with troll poetry and in turn has shown us her tattoo.

Jamin Still spent his formative years on Air Force bases all over America and England before finally settling in the great state of Kansas. He took ten years to finish college (during which he changed his mind multiple times, electing to study environmental science, graphic design, medieval English literature, medieval art history, criminal justice, and painting). He then changed his mind again and became a pastor—but the desire to write and paint was so strong that in 2014 he decided to—you guessed it—change his mind and pursue creative endeavors full time. He does not intend to change career paths again until he changes his mind.

Jennifer Trafton is the author of *The Rise and Fall of Mount Majestic*, a nominee for the 2012 Volunteer State Book Award. She teaches creative writing to kids, is hard at work on her next book, and would love nothing more than to live on a sailboat with a dancing giraffe. *(www.JenniferTrafton.com)*

Walter Wangerin, Jr. is the National Book Award-winning author of *The Book of the Dun Cow*, *Ragman & Other Cries of Faith*, *Letters from the Land of Cancer*, and the forthcoming *Everlasting Is the Past* (Rabbit Room Press

2015). He is also well-known for blowing minds as the keynote speaker at Hutchmoot 2010. *(www.WaltWangerinJr.org)*

CHRIS YOKEL teaches writing and literature to college and high school students and serves as Church Assistant for Worship, Liturgy, and Teaching at Christ Covenant Church in Fall River, Massachusetts. He lives with his wife Jen in a tiny apartment called The Flet. Together they enjoy reading, writing poetry, and exploring the cities, coasts, and forests of New England. He also enjoys the new *Hobbit* movies; this can and will be held against him.

JEN ROSE YOKEL has worked in Christian radio for over ten years, and currently does social media and production for The Q 90.1 in Worcester, Massachusetts. She has also written numerous pieces for JesusFreakHideout and other publications. She is currently a Florida girl adjusting to life in New England with her husband Chris, where we trust she will train him in the errors of his hobbitual ways.

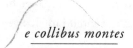

e collibus montes

RABBIT ROOM
— PRESS —

Fostering Spiritual Formation and Christ-centered Community
Through Story, Art, and Music

— *The* —
RABBIT ROOM

est. 2006

www.RABBITROOM.com

Also available from Rabbit Room Press:

THE MOLEHILL, VOLS. 1 & 2

EVERLASTING IS THE PAST (Spring 2015)
by Walter Wangerin, Jr.

THE WARDEN AND THE WOLF KING
by Andrew Peterson

MONSTER IN THE HOLLOWS
by Andrew Peterson

SUBJECTS WITH OBJECTS
by DKM and Jonathan Richter

REAL LOVE FOR REAL LIFE
by Andi Ashworth

BEHOLD THE LAMB OF GOD
by Russ Ramsey

THE CYMBAL CRASHING CLOUDS
by Ben Shive

THE FIDDLER'S GUN and FIDDLER'S GREEN
by A. S. Peterson

CPSIA information can be obtained
at www.ICGtesting.com
Printed in the USA
JSHW042346130722
27985JS00003BA/10